LEVEL 1 Supplemental
ANSWER BOOK

By Glory St. Germain ARCT RMT MYCC UMTC &
Shelagh McKibbon-U'Ren RMT UMTC

The LEVEL 1 Supplemental Workbook is designed to be completed after the Prep 1 Rudiments and Prep Level Supplemental Workbook.

GSG MUSIC
Enriching Lives Through Music Education

ISBN: 978-1-927641-52-1

The Ultimate Music Theory™ Program

The Ultimate Music Theory™ Program lays the foundation of music theory education.

The focus of the Ultimate Music Theory Program is to simplify complex concepts and show the relativity of these concepts with practical application. This program is designed to help teachers and students discover the excitement and benefits of a sound music theory education.

The Ultimate Music Theory Program is based on a proven approach to the study of music theory that follows the *"must have"* Learning Principles to develop effective learning for all learning styles.

The Ultimate Music Theory™ Program and Supplemental Workbooks help students prepare for nationally recognized theory examinations including the Royal Conservatory of Music.

Respect Copyright - Copyright 2017 Gloryland Publishing
All rights reserved. No part of this publication may be reproduced or transmitted in any form or by any means, electronic or mechanical, including photocopying, recording, or any information storage and retrieval system, without permission in writing from the author/publisher.

* Resources - An annotated list is available at UltimateMusicTheory.com under Free Resources.

Library and Archives Canada Cataloguing in Publication
UMT Supplemental Series / Glory St. Germain and Shelagh McKibbon-U'Ren

Gloryland Publishing - UMT Supplemental Series Answer Books:

GP-SPLA	ISBN: 978-1-927641-51-4	UMT Supplemental Prep Level Answer Book
GP-SL1A	ISBN: 978-1-927641-52-1	UMT Supplemental Level 1 Answer Book
GP-SL2A	ISBN: 978-1-927641-53-8	UMT Supplemental Level 2 Answer Book
GP-SL3A	ISBN: 978-1-927641-54-5	UMT Supplemental Level 3 Answer Book
GP-SL4A	ISBN: 978-1-927641-55-2	UMT Supplemental Level 4 Answer Book
GP-SL5A	ISBN: 978-1-927641-56-9	UMT Supplemental Level 5 Answer Book
GP-SL6A	ISBN: 978-1-927641-57-6	UMT Supplemental Level 6 Answer Book
GP-SL7A	ISBN: 978-1-927641-58-3	UMT Supplemental Level 7 Answer Book
GP-SL8A	ISBN: 978-1-927641-59-0	UMT Supplemental Level 8 Answer Book
GP-SCLA	ISBN: 978-1-927641-60-6	UMT Supplemental Complete Level Answer Book

Ultimate Music Theory
LEVEL 1 Supplemental

Table of Contents

Ultimate Music Theory	The Story of UMT... Meet So-La & Ti-Do	4
Comparison Chart	Level 1	6
Two Ledger Lines	Treble Staff and Bass Staff	8
Pitches on the Staff	Same and Different	10
Steps and Skips	Grand Staff	12
Writing Accidentals	Ledger Line Notes	14
Half Step & Whole Step	Same and Different Letter Names	15
Interval of a Second	Whole Step	19
Major Tetrachords	Pattern of Whole Steps and Half Steps	20
Major Scales	Accidentals and Tonic & Dominant Scale Degrees	21
Key Signatures	Major Scales	22
Major Scales	Major Scales with Accidentals or with Key Signatures	23
Minor Scale	A Minor Scale Natural Form	24
Tonic Triads	Solid/Blocked and Broken	25
Common Time	Tied Notes and Values	26
Music Theory Game	Bunk Bed Bar Lines!	27
Motives & Patterns	Repeated Motive & Patterns	28
Composing Patterns	Rhythmic & Melodic	30
Melody Writing	Repeated Notes, Stepwise Motion & Key Signatures	32
Analysis and Terms	ICE, Sight Reading - Brave Little Mouse	34
Orchestral Instruments	Story Telling Through Sound	36
Music & Story Telling	Peter and the Wolf & Carnival of the Animals	38
Theory Exam	Level 1	41
Certificate	Completion of Level 1	48

Score: 60 - 69 Pass; 70 - 79 Honors; 80 - 89 First Class Honors; 90 - 100 First Class Honors with Distinction

Ultimate Music Theory: *The Way to Score Success!*

Ultimate Music Theory

Workbooks, Exams, Answers, Online Courses, App & More!

A Proven Step-by-Step System to Learn Theory Faster - from Beginner to Advanced.

Innovative techniques designed to develop a complete understanding of music theory, to enhance sight reading, ear training, creativity, composition and musical expression.

All UMT Series have matching Answer Books!

The UMT Rudiments Series - Beginner A, Beginner B, Beginner C, Prep 1, Prep 2, Basic, Intermediate, Advanced & Complete (All-In-One)

- ♪ 12 Lessons, Review Tests, and a Final Exam to develop confidence
- ♪ Music Theory Guide & Chart for fast and easy reference of theory concepts
- ♪ 80 Flashcards for fun drills to dramatically increase retention & comprehension

Rudiments Exam Series - Preparatory, Basic, Intermediate & Advanced

- ♪ 8 Exams plus UMT Tips on How to Score 100% on Theory Exams

Each Rudiments Workbook correlates to a Supplemental Workbook.

The UMT Supplemental Series - Prep Level, Level 1, Level 2, Level 3, Level 4, Level 5, Level 6, Level 7, Level 8 & Complete (All-In-One) Level

- ♪ Form & Analysis and Music History - Composers, Eras & Musical Styles
- ♪ Melody Writing using ICE - Imagine, Compose & Explore
- ♪ 12 Lessons, Review Tests, Final Exam and 80 Flashcards for quick study

Supplemental Exam Series - Level 5, Level 6, Level 7 & Level 8

- ♪ 8 Exams to successfully prepare for nationally recognized Theory Exams

UMT Online Courses, Music Theory App & More

- ♪ UMT Certification Course, Teachers Membership & Elite Educator Program
- ♪ Ultimate Music Theory App correlates to the Rudiments Workbooks
- ♪ Free Resources - Teachers Guide, Music Theory Blogs, videos & downloads

Go To: UltimateMusicTheory.com

At Ultimate Music Theory we are passionate about helping teachers and students experience the joy of teaching and learning music by creating the most effective music theory materials on the planet!

Introducing the Ultimate Music Theory Family!

So-La

Meet So-La! So-La loves to sing and dance.

She is expressive, creative and loves to tell stories through music!

So-La feels music in her heart. She loves to teach, compose and perform.

Ti-Do

Meet Ti-Do! Ti-Do loves to count and march.

He is rhythmic, consistent and loves the rules of music theory!

Ti-Do feels music in his hands and feet. He loves to analyze, share tips and conduct.

So-La & Ti-Do will guide you through Mastering Music Theory!

Enriching Lives Through Music Education

The Ultimate Music Theory™ Comparison Chart to the 2016 Royal Conservatory of Music Theory Syllabus.
Level 1

The Ultimate Music Theory™ Rudiments Workbooks, Supplemental Workbooks and Exams prepare students for successful completion of the Royal Conservatory of Music Theory Levels.

UMT Prep 1 Rudiments Workbook plus the PREP LEVEL Supplemental = RCM Preparatory Level.
♫ Note: Additional completion of the LEVEL 1 Supplemental Workbook = RCM Theory Level 1.

RCM Level 1 Theory Concept

Required Keys:
- C Major and a minor, F Major, G Major

Pitch and Notation:
- Notes up to and including two ledger line above and below the Treble & Bass Staff

- Measure Numbers
- Accidentals: Sharp, Flat and Natural

Rhythm and Meter
- Notes: dotted half notes
- Time Signatures: 2/4, 3/4, 4/4 (Common Time)

Intervals
- Half Steps - using the same letter name or using different letter names
- Whole Steps

- Melodic and Harmonic intervals up to and including an octave (numerical size only)

Scales and Scale Degree Names
- Scales using Key Signatures and/or Accidentals:
  - C Major, G Major and F Major
  - a minor scale, natural form
- Scale Degree Names: Tonic and Dominant

Chords
- Tonic Triad of C Major, G Major, F Major and of a minor (Root Position, solid/blocked and broken)
- Triad Structure: Root, Third, Fifth

Ultimate Music Theory Prep 1 Workbook

Keys Covered:
- C Major and a minor; F Major and d minor; G Major and e minor

Pitch and Notation Covered:
* Workbook pages - Two Ledger Lines - Treble Staff & Bass Staff
* Workbook pages - Pitches on the Staff - Same and Different
* Workbook pages - Steps and Skips - Grand Staff

- Measure Numbers

- Accidentals: Sharp, Flat and Natural
* Workbook page - Writing Accidentals on Ledger Line Notes

Rhythm and Meter Covered
- Notes: dotted half notes, Time Signatures: 2/4, 3/4 and 4/4
*Workbook pages - Common Time, Game - Bunk Bed Bar Lines!

Intervals Covered
- Half Steps/Semitones - using same or different letter names
* Workbook pages - Half Step (Same and Different letter names)
- Whole Steps/Whole Tones
* Workbook pages - Whole Step - Different Letter Names
- Melodic and Harmonic intervals up to and including an octave (numerical size only)

Scales and Scale Degree Names Covered
*Workbook page - Major Tetrachords
*Workbook pages - Major Scales (C, G, F) using Accidentals
*Workbook pages - Major Scales (C, G, F) using a Key Signature
*Workbook page - minor scale - Natural Form
- Scale Degree Names: Tonic, Mediant and Dominant

Chords Covered
- Tonic Triads of C, F & G Major, a, d & e minor
*Workbook page - Tonic Triads - Solid/Blocked and Broken
- Triad Structure: Tonic (Root), Mediant (Third), Dominant (Fifth)

* Supplemental Workbook Pages - New concepts introduced in the 2016 RCM Syllabus.

RCM Level 1 Theory Concept (Continued)

Melody and Composition
- Recurring Motives (rhythmic and/or melodic patterns)
- Composition of a Short Melody in a Major Key with a given rhythm, using stepwise motion and repeated notes, ending on the Tonic

Analysis
- Identification of concepts from this level and the previous level within short music examples
- identification of stepwise motion and non-stepwise motion within short music examples

Musical Terms and Signs
- Tempo, Dynamics and Articulation

Music History/Appreciation
- Guided Listening: Carnival of the Animals - The Elephant; Kangaroos; Aquarium and The Swan
   Listening Focus: Featured Instruments
Relationship of Music to the descriptive titles
- Guided Listening: Peter and the Wolf
Listening Focus: Featured Instruments
Musical depiction of the storyline and characters

Examination
(No Level 1 Theory Exam)

Ultimate Music Theory Prep 1 Workbook (Continued)

Melody and Composition Covered
*Workbook pages - Motive - Rhythmic Pattern and Melodic Pattern Recurring Motive - Identifying Patterns, Composing - Patterns
Workbook pages - Composing a Melody (Major key, given rhythm, using stepwise motion and repeated notes, ending on the Tonic)
*Melody Writing - Repeated Notes & Stepwise Motion
*Melody Writing - Key Signatures & Time Signatures

Analysis Covered
- Identification of concepts from this level and the previous level within short music examples
- identification of step, skip and repeated motion within short music examples * Workbook page - Analysis, Terms and Sight Reading

Musical Terms and Signs Covered
*Workbook page - Common Time and Tied Notes

Music History/Appreciation Covered
*Workbook page - Story Telling Through Music - Carnival of the Animals by Camille Saint-Saëns
   Instruments: Double Bass, Piano, Glass Harmonica and Cello
*Workbook page - Story Telling Through Music - Peter and the Wolf by Sergei Prokofiev
*Workbook page - Orchestral Instruments
*Workbook page - Story Telling Through Sound

Review Tests & Final Exam
- 12 Accumulative Review Tests (1 with each of the 12 Lessons)
*UMT LEVEL 1 THEORY EXAM

UltimateMusicTheoryApp.com - Over 7000 Flashcards including audio! 6 Subjects: Beginner - Prep, Basic, Intermediate, Advanced, Ear Training & Music Trivia (including History).

Beginner Music Theory App Subject - Use with the Prep 1 and Prep 2 Workbooks

12 Decks - 1,325 Cards - See, hear and identify notes on the staff, scales, triads and musical terms. Learn notation including note and rest values, Key Signatures, 4/4 Simple Time & more!

1 - Notation, Landmarks and Ledger Lines

2 - Note & Rest Values and Intervals

3 - Simple Time Signatures

4 - Semitones, Whole tones & Accidentals

5 - Major scales - 2 sharps & 2 flats

6 - Natural minor scales - 2 sharps & 2 flats

7 - Key Signatures - 2 sharps & 2 flats

8 - Key Signatures on the Grand Staff

9 - Major Triads - solid and broken

10 - Harmonic minor scales

11 - Melodic minor scales

12 - Analysis and Musical Terms

TWO LEDGER LINES - TREBLE STAFF

Ledger Lines are short lines used to extend the staff as needed for notes written above or below the **Treble Clef**. Ledger lines must be equal distance from the staff.

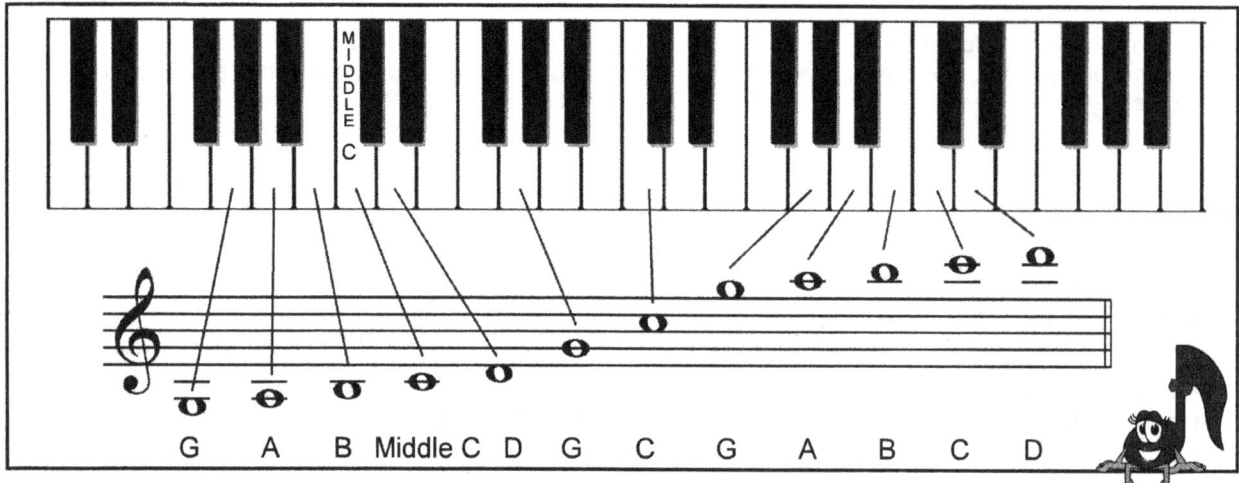

1. a) Copy the following notes stepping up from the G below Middle C.
   b) Name the notes.

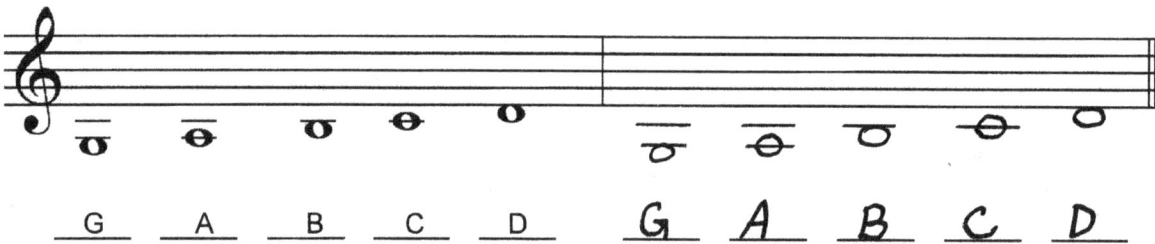

2. a) Copy the following notes stepping down from the D above the Treble Staff.
   b) Name the notes.

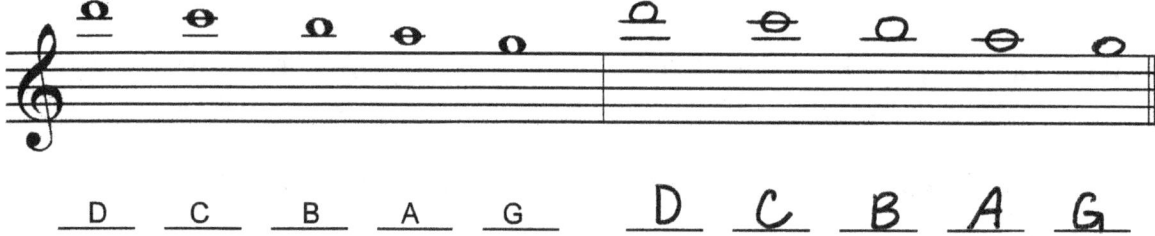

3. Name the following notes in the Treble Clef.

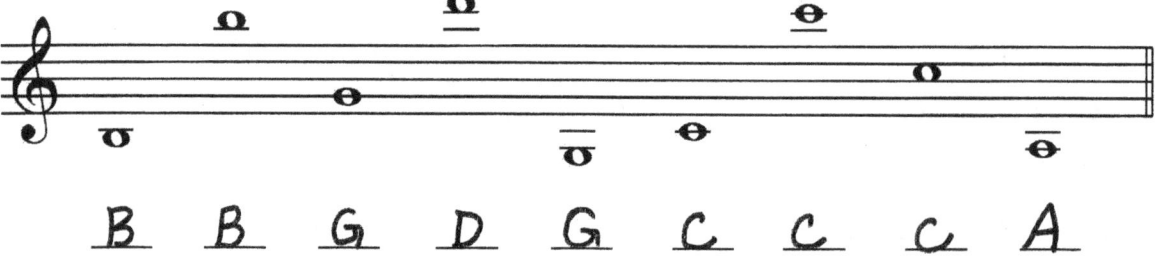

TWO LEDGER LINES - BASS STAFF

Ledger Lines are short lines used to extend the staff as needed for notes written above or below the **Bass Clef**. Use your UMT Ruler to draw perfectly spaced Ledger Lines.

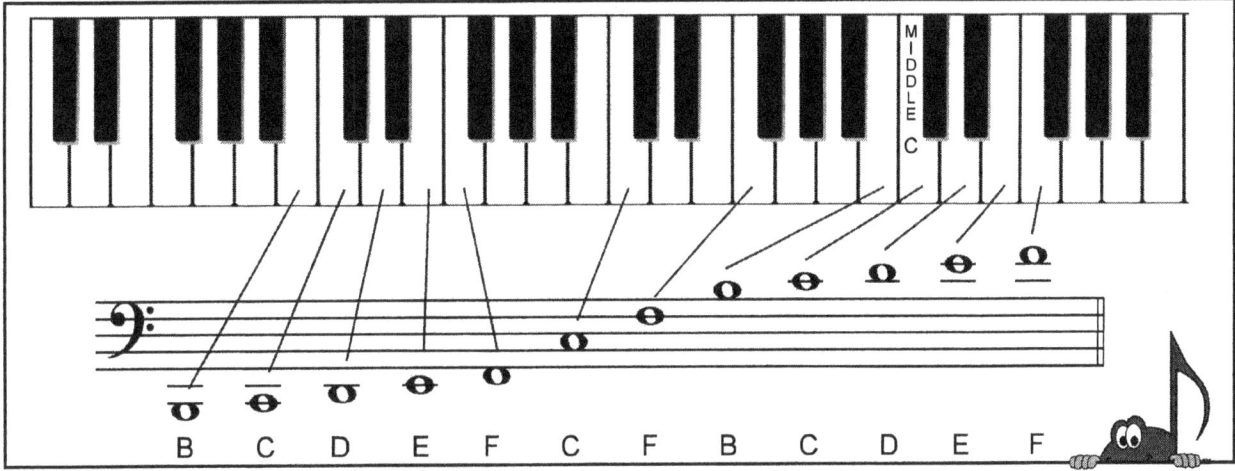

1. a) Copy the following notes stepping up from the low B below the Bass Staff.
   b) Name the notes.

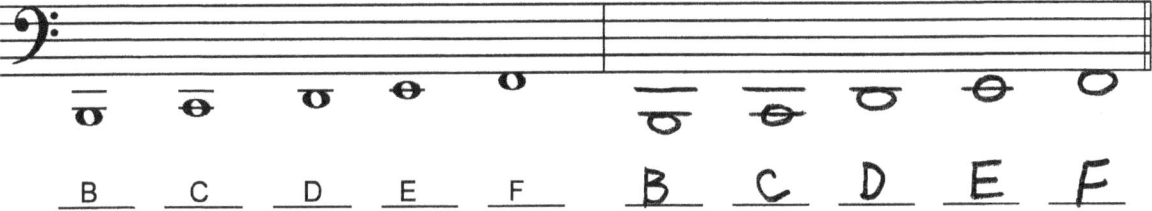

B C D E F B C D E F

2. a) Copy the following notes stepping down from the F above the Bass Staff.
   b) Name the notes.

F E D C B F E D C B

3. Name the following notes in the Bass Clef.

D D C F B E E F C

SAME PITCH - DIFFERENT STAFF

Using Ledger Lines, notes can be written at the **same pitch** in the Treble Staff and in the Bass Staff.

♫ **Ti-Do Tip:** Ledger line notes written closer to the Treble Staff are used for Treble Clef notes.
Ledger line notes written closer to the Bass Staff are used for Bass Clef notes.

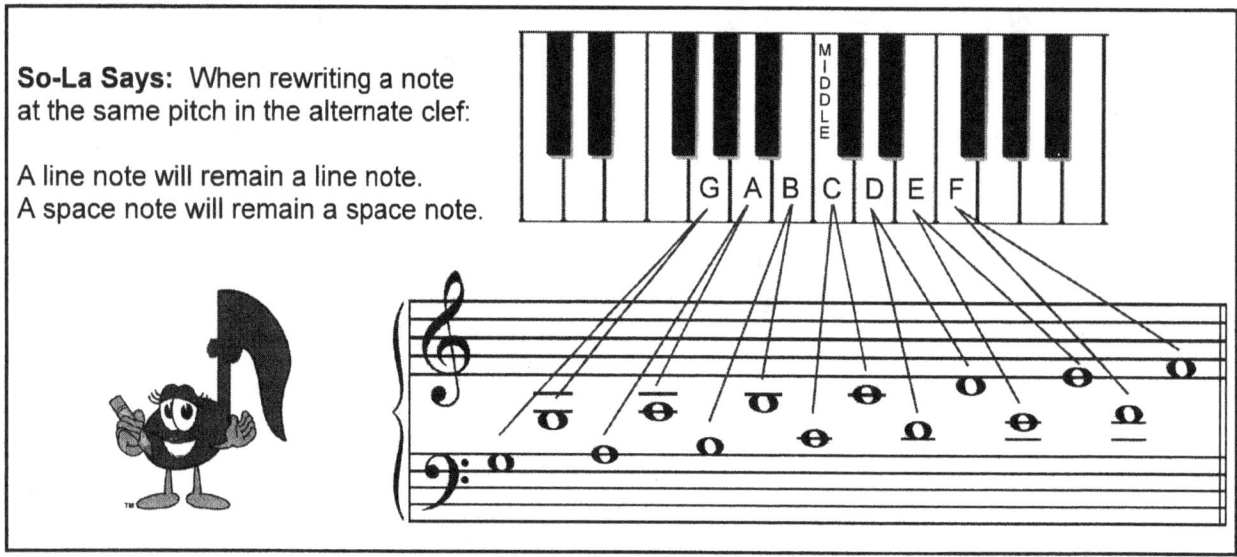

So-La Says: When rewriting a note at the same pitch in the alternate clef:

A line note will remain a line note.
A space note will remain a space note.

♫ **Ti-Do Tip:** Two notes written at the same pitch but in alternate clefs will sound the same.

1. a) Name the following notes.
   b) Circle the correct pitch pattern below.

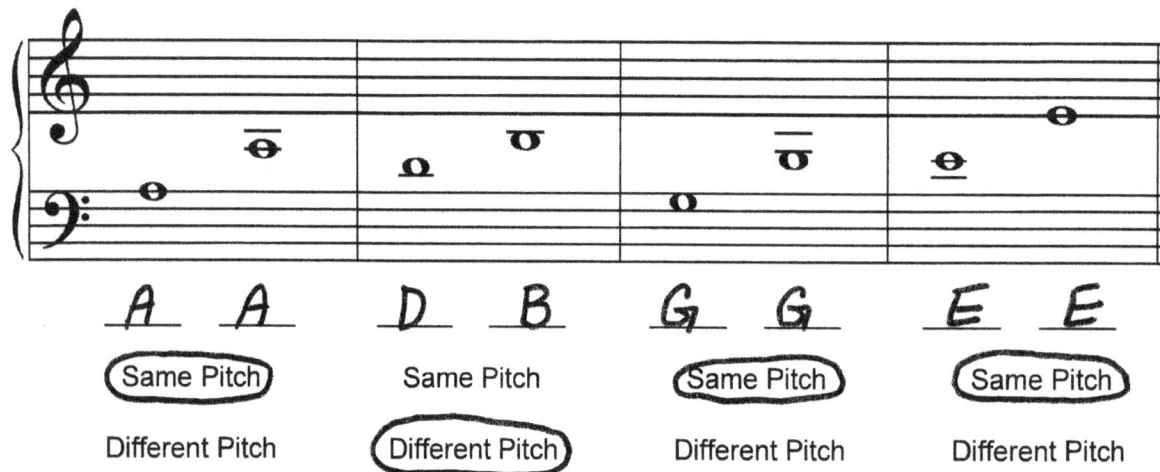

♫ Ti-Do Time:

LISTEN as your Teacher plays the 2 note patterns in Exercise #1. Without looking at the music, identify if the pitch (sound) is at the Same Pitch or at a Different Pitch.

DIFFERENT PITCHES - SAME LETTER NAMES

Each letter name of the Musical Alphabet can be written at **different pitches** on the Grand Staff.

Each letter name can also be written at the same pitch but in the alternate (other) clef.

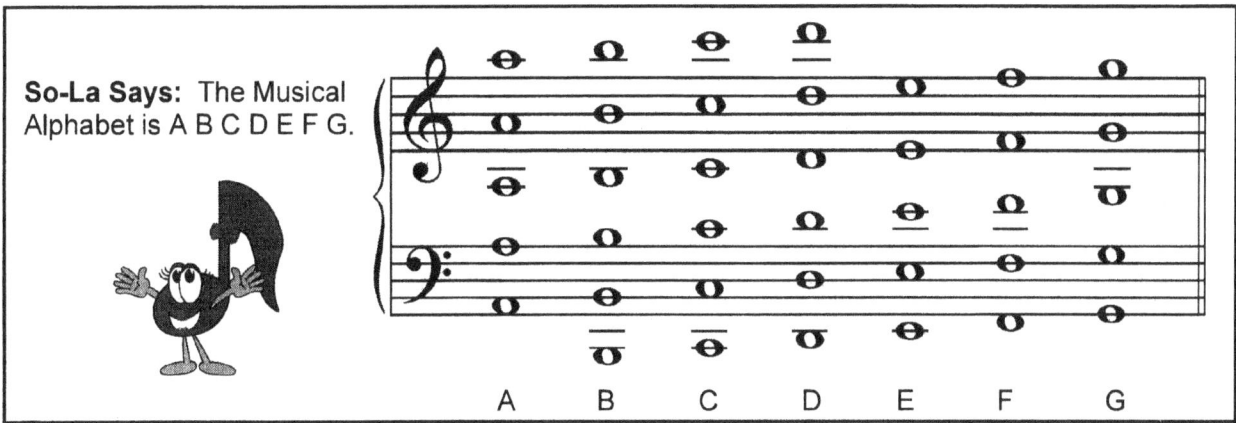

1. a) Name each note.
   b) In each measure, circle the 2 notes that are written at the same pitch but in the alternate clef.

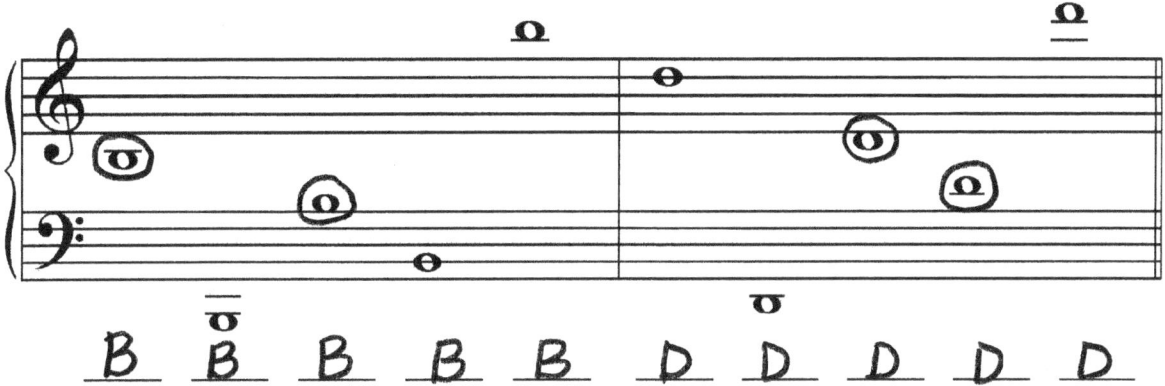

♪ **Ti-Do Tip:** An Octave is the distance of 8 notes. The distance between one note and the next note with the same letter name (going up or going down) is an Octave (8 notes).

2. In each measure, write three more notes for each letter name. Use whole notes. Each note must be at a different pitch.

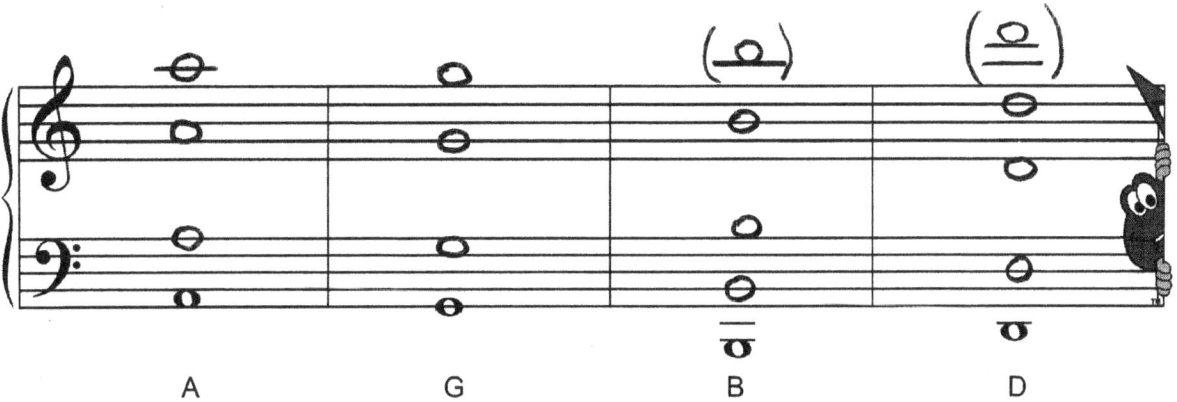

UltimateMusicTheory.com © Copyright 2017 Gloryland Publishing. All Rights Reserved.

STEPS - GRAND STAFF

A **Step** may step up or step down in pitch. The lower the note on the Grand Staff, the lower the pitch. As notes step up the Grand Staff, the sound gets higher in pitch.

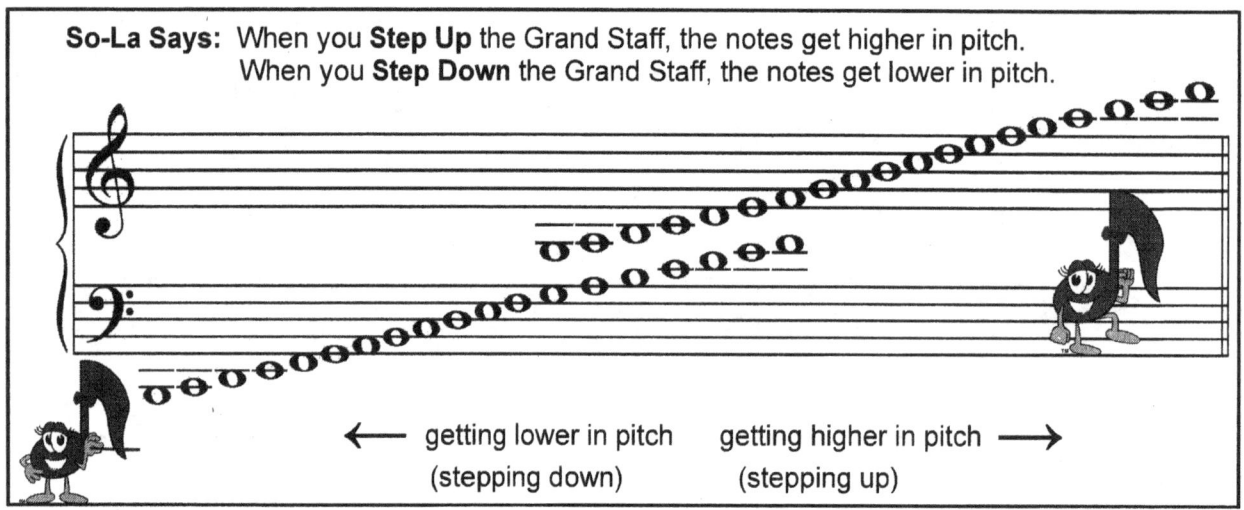

♫ **Ti-Do Tip:** A step is written from a line note to the next space note, or from a space note to the next line note. A step may step up or step down.

1. a) Following the Direction Arrow, draw a whole note a step up or a step down from each note.
   b) Name the notes.

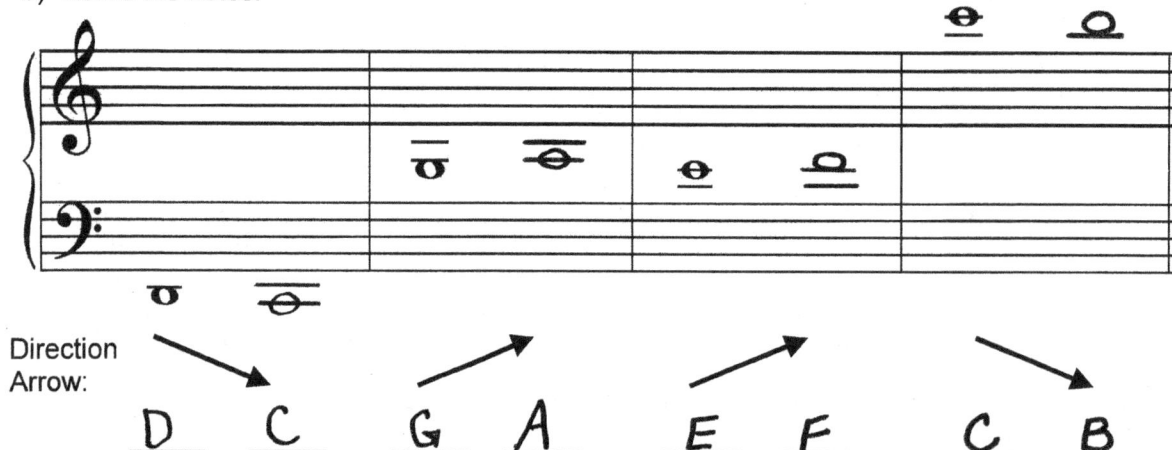

♫ **Ti-Do Time:**

LISTEN as your Teacher plays notes from the Example Box. Without looking at the music, identify if the pitch (sound) is Stepping Up or Stepping Down.

LISTEN as your Teacher plays the 2 note patterns in Exercise #1. Without looking at the music, identify if the pitch (sound) is a Step Up or a Step Down.

SKIPS - GRAND STAFF

A **Skip** may skip up or skip down in pitch. A skip is written from a line note to the next line note (skipping a space) or a space note to the next space note (skipping a line).

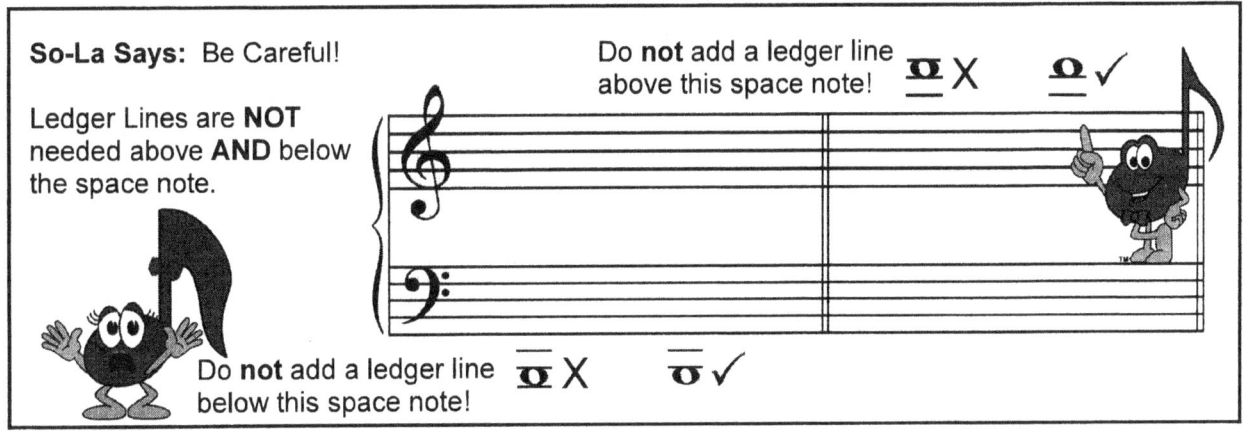

♪ **Ti-Do Tip:** Use your UMT Ruler to draw a straight and evenly spaced Ledger Line!

1. Identify if the Ledger Line Skips are Correct or Incorrect.

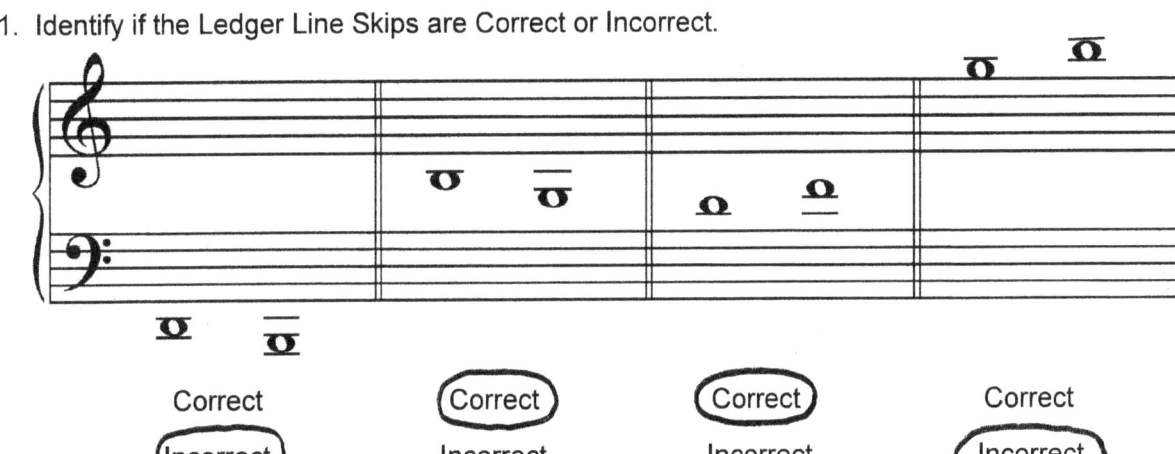

2. a) Following the Direction Arrow, draw a whole note a skip up or a skip down from each note.
   b) Name the notes.

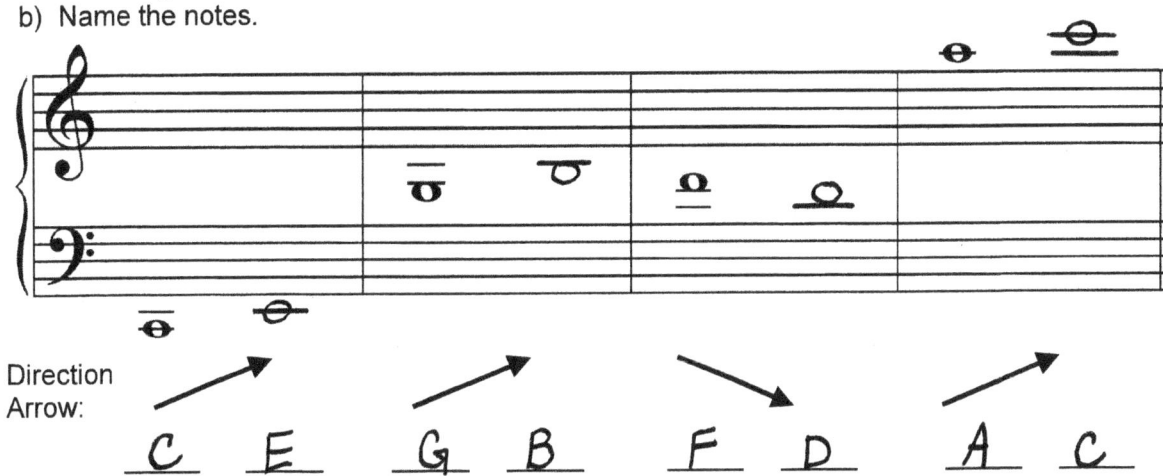

WRITING ACCIDENTALS on LEDGER LINE NOTES

Accidentals (sharp, flat or natural) are written in front of (before) the note and after the letter name.

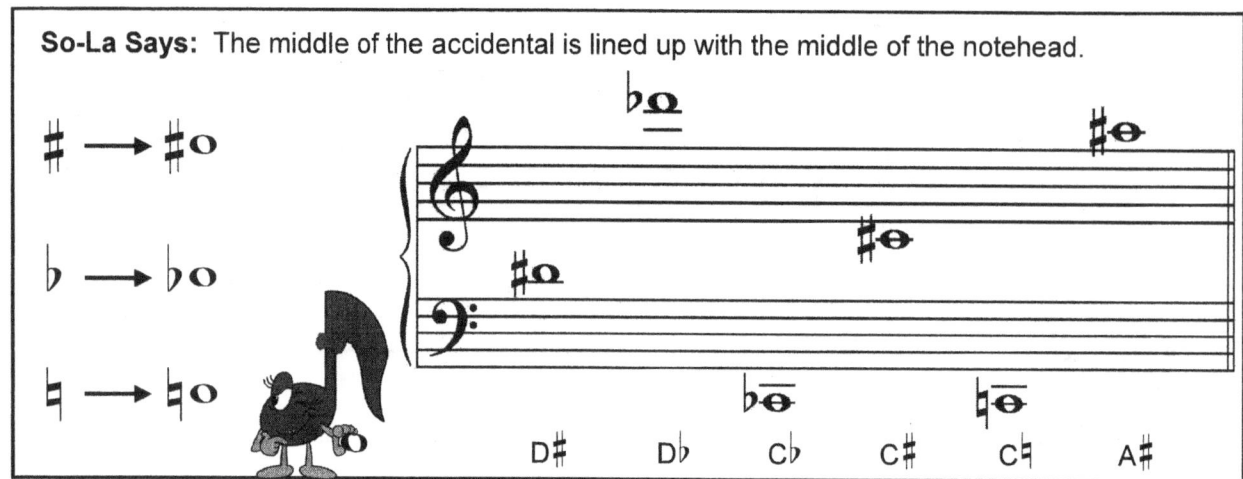

♪ **Ti-Do Tip:** When the note is written using a ledger line, the ledger line is not extended through the accidental (sharp, flat or natural).

1. Add the correct accidental to each whole note.

2. Write the following notes using ledger lines. Use whole notes.

HALF STEPS (Semitones) and WHOLE STEPS (Whole Tones)

A **Half Step** (Semitone) is the smallest distance between two keys. On the Keyboard, a Half Step is from one key (black or white) to the next key, with no key in between.

So-La Says: A **Half Step** will go from:

A Black Key to a White Key.
A White Key to a Black Key.
A White Key to a White Key.

1. a) On the keyboard, add the line to indicate a half step (semitone) above each of the given lines.
   b) Indicate whether the half step (semitone) is going to a white key or a black key.

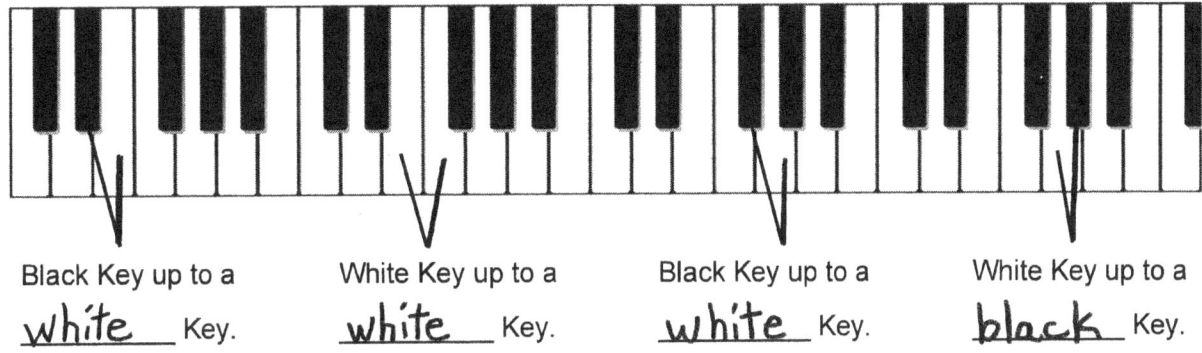

Black Key up to a _white_ Key.   White Key up to a _white_ Key.   Black Key up to a _white_ Key.   White Key up to a _black_ Key.

A **Whole Step** (Whole Tone) is equal to two half steps (semitones). On the Keyboard, a Whole Step is from one key to the next key, with one key (black or white) in between.

So-La Says: A **Whole Step** will go from:

A White Key to a White Key.
A Black Key to a Black Key.
A Black Key to a White Key.
A White Key to a Black Key.

2. a) On the keyboard, add the line to indicate a whole step below each of the given lines.
   b) Indicate whether the whole step (whole tone) is going to a white key or a black key.

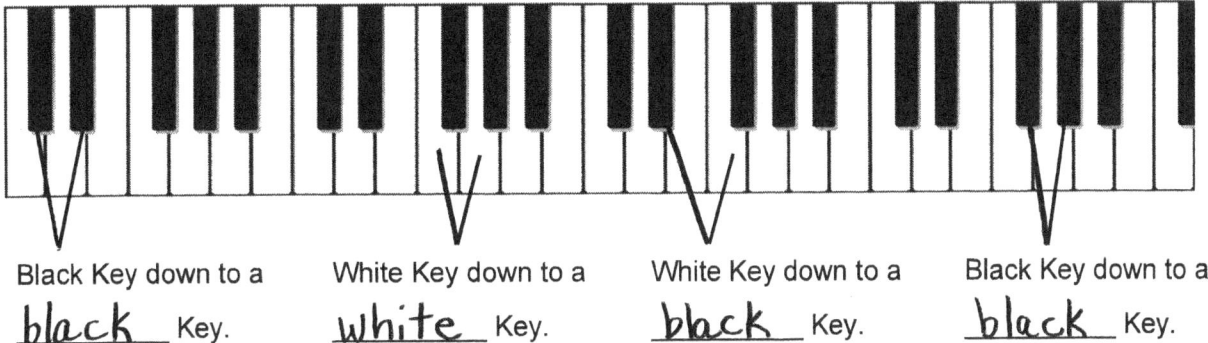

Black Key down to a _black_ Key.   White Key down to a _white_ Key.   White Key down to a _black_ Key.   Black Key down to a _black_ Key.

HALF STEPS - SAME LETTER NAMES

A **Half Step** (Semitone) is the smallest musical interval in sound. A half step is the distance between two neighboring (next door) notes.

A Half Step can be written using the **same letter name**. This is called a **Chromatic Half Step**.

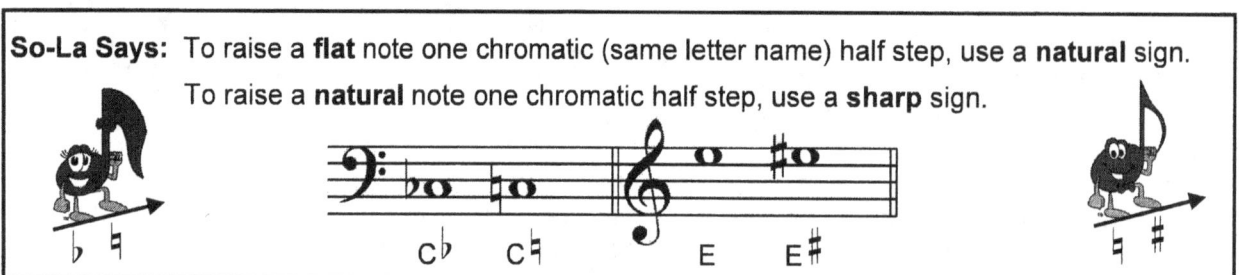

So-La Says: To raise a **flat** note one chromatic (same letter name) half step, use a **natural** sign.
To raise a **natural** note one chromatic half step, use a **sharp** sign.

♪ **Ti-Do Tip:** To write a half step using the same letter name, write the note first (on the same line or in the same space) and then add the accidental to raise or lower the pitch.

1. a) Raise the following notes one half step using the same letter name. Use whole notes.
   b) Name the notes.

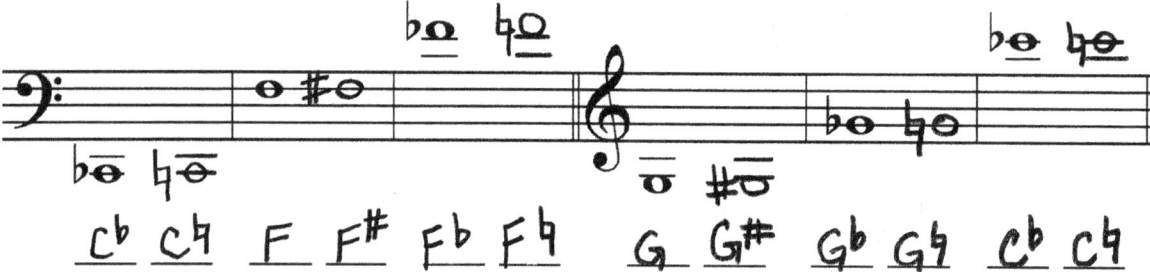

C♭ C♮   F F♯   F♭ F♮   G G♯   G♭ G♮   C♭ C♮

So-La Says: To lower a **sharp** note one chromatic (same letter name) half step, use a **natural** sign.
To lower a **natural** note one chromatic half step, use a **flat** sign.

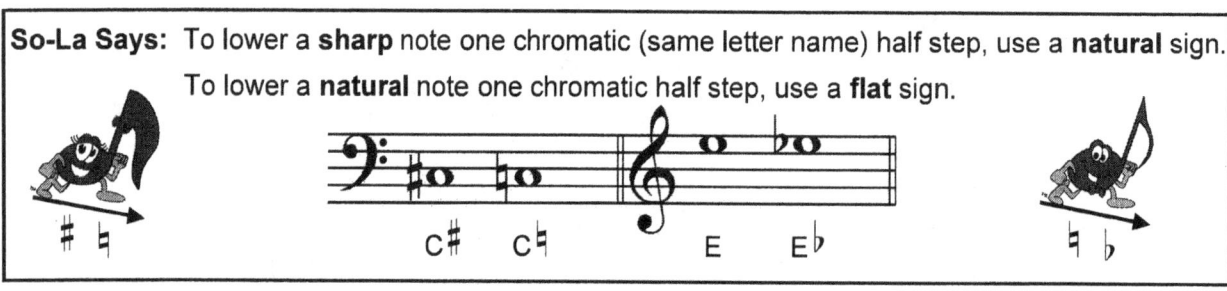

2. a) Lower the following notes one half step using the same letter name. Use whole notes.
   b) Name the notes.

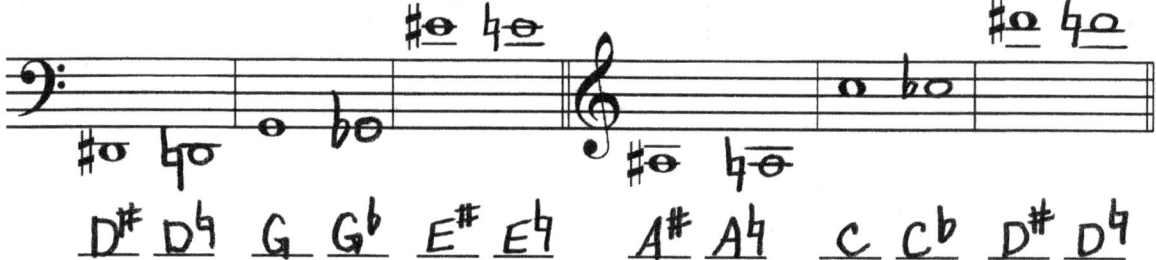

D♯ D♮   G G♭   E♯ E♮   A♯ A♮   C C♭   D♯ D♮

HALF STEPS - DIFFERENT LETTER NAMES

A **Half Step** (Semitone) is the distance between one note and the very next note, above or below, black or white, no key in between.

A Half Step can be written using a **different letter name**. This is called a **Diatonic Half Step.**

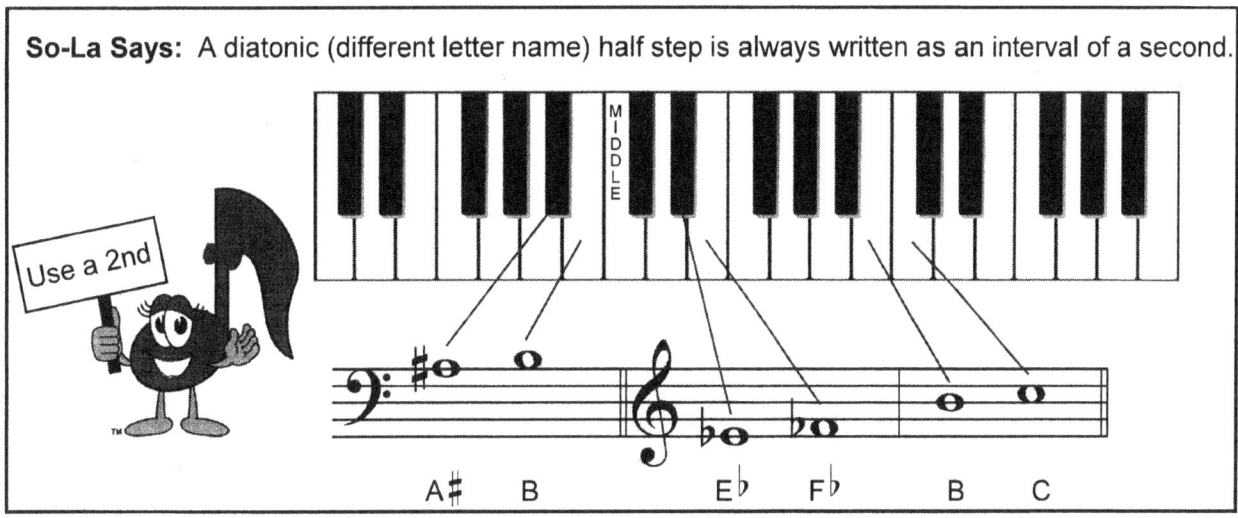

So-La Says: A diatonic (different letter name) half step is always written as an interval of a second.

♪ **Ti-Do Tip:** To write a half step using a different letter name, write the note a 2nd above or below the given note and then add an accidental (if necessary) to create the half step.

1. a) Raise the following notes one half step using a different letter name. Use whole notes.
   b) Name the notes.

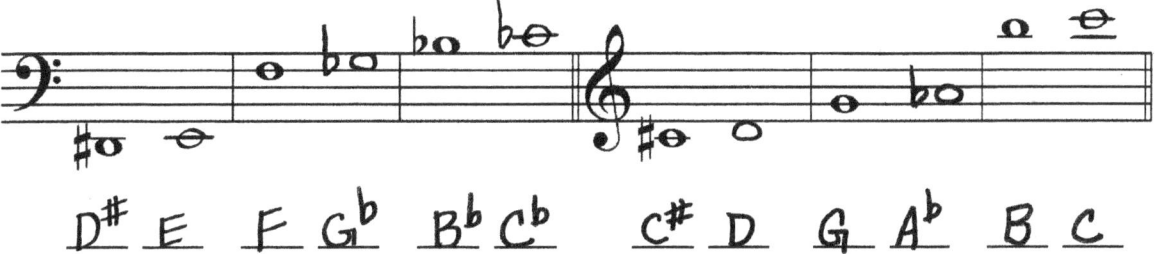

D♯ E F G♭ B♭ C♭ C♯ D G A♭ B C

2. a) Lower the following notes one half step using a different letter name. Use whole notes.
   b) Name the notes.

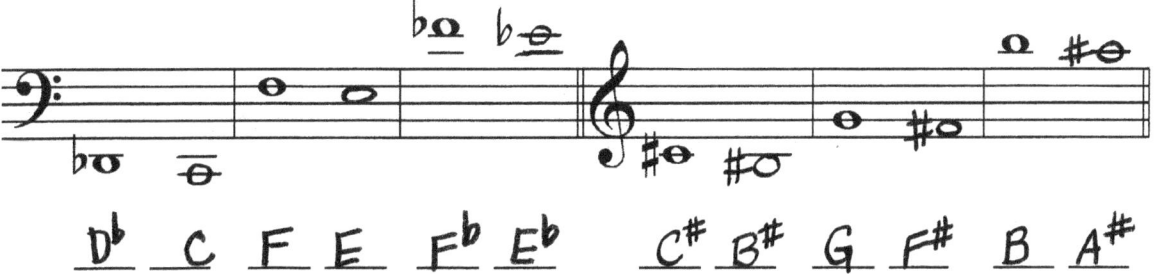

D♭ C F E F♭ E♭ C♯ B♯ G F♯ B A♯

WHOLE STEPS - DIFFERENT LETTER NAMES

A **Whole Step** (Whole Tone) is equal to two half steps (semitones). On the Staff, a Whole Step is usually written as an interval of a second using **different letter names**.

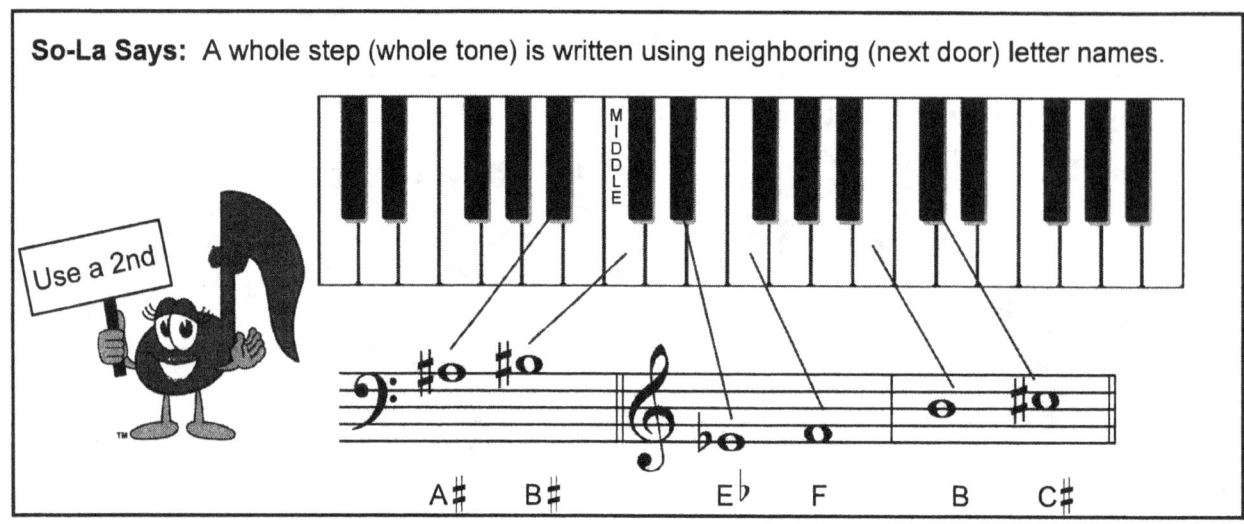

Ti-Do Tip: To write a whole step, write the note a 2nd above or below the given note and then add an accidental (if necessary) to skip one key, black or white.

1. a) Write the note that is a whole step (whole tone) above each given note. Use whole notes.
   b) Name the notes.

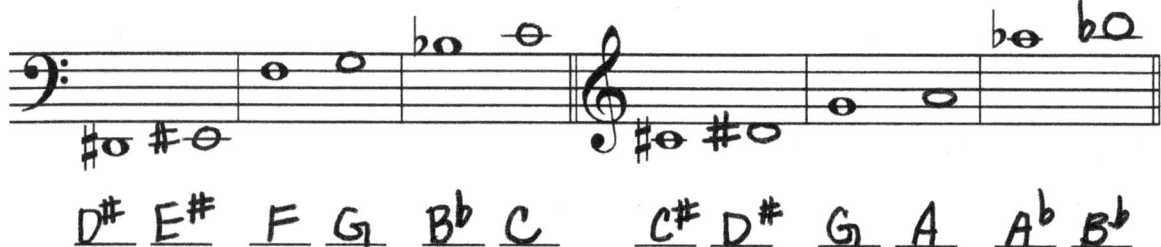

D♯ E♯   F G   B♭ C   C♯ D♯   G A   A♭ B♭

2. a) Write the note that is a whole step (whole tone) below each given note. Use whole notes.
   b) Name the notes.

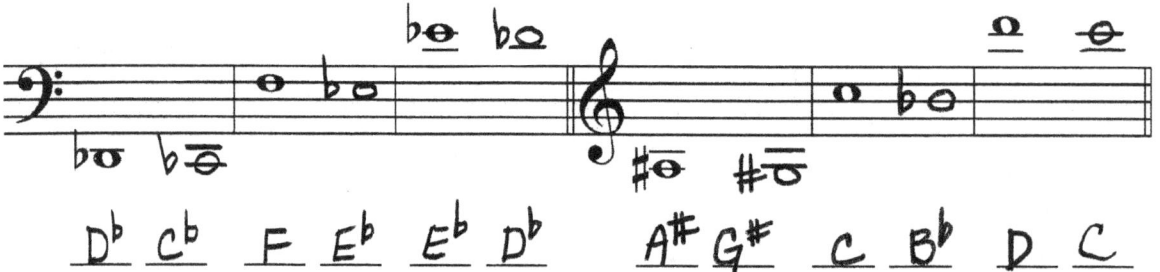

D♭ C♭   F E♭   E♭ D♭   A♯ G♯   C B♭   D C

WHOLE STEPS - INTERVAL OF A SECOND

A **Whole Step** (Whole Tone) using neighboring letter names is written as an **interval of a second**.

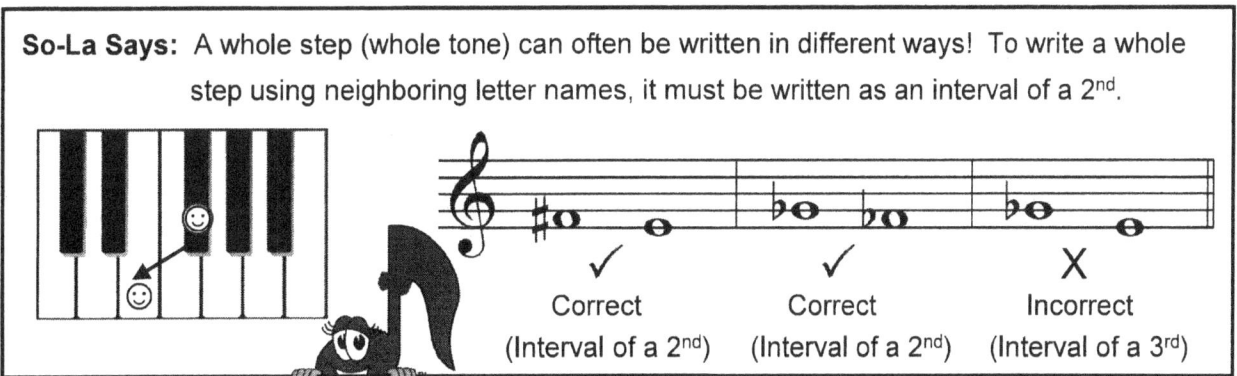

So-La Says: A whole step (whole tone) can often be written in different ways! To write a whole step using neighboring letter names, it must be written as an interval of a 2nd.

♪ **Ti-Do Time:** Play the notes in the Example. Are they at the same pitch or at different pitches?

Two notes may sound like a whole step when played, even though they are written differently.

1. a) Name the notes. Draw a line from each note on the staff to the corresponding key on the keyboard (at the correct pitch).
   b) Identify if the whole step (written using neighboring letter names) is Correct or Incorrect.

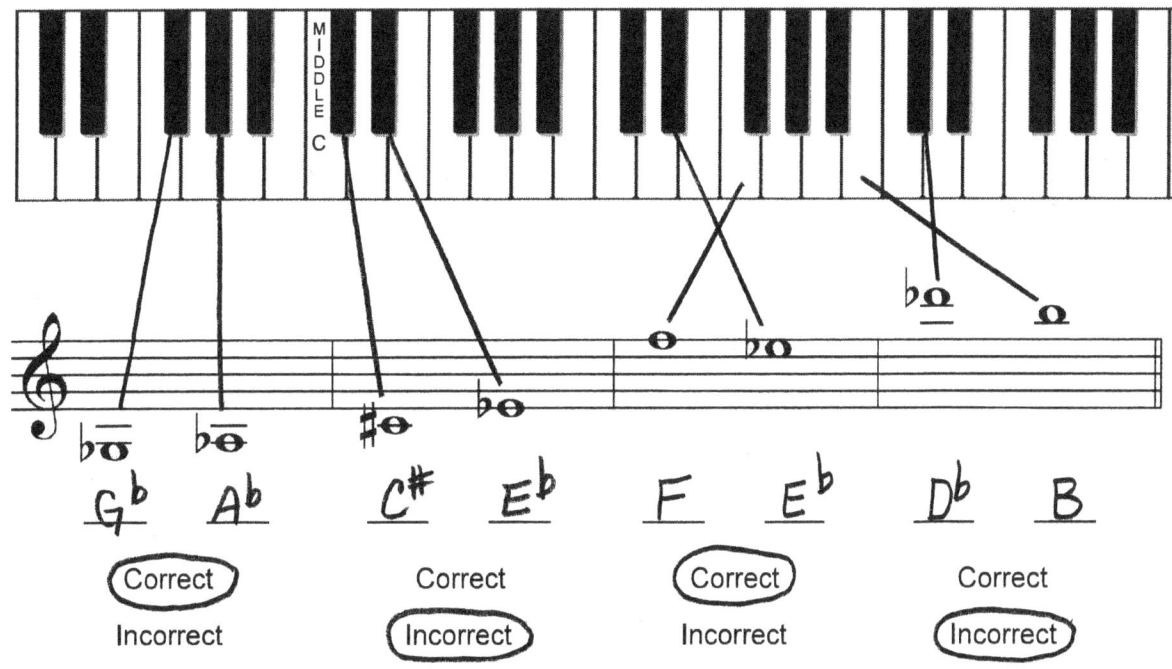

♪ **Ti-Do Time:** LISTEN as your Teacher plays whole steps from the Exercise. Without looking at the music, identify if the pitch (sound) is Stepping Up or Stepping Down.

MAJOR TETRACHORDS

A **Tetrachord** is a series of four notes in alphabetical order. Tetra means four and chord means a pattern of notes. A **Major Tetrachord** is a series of 4 notes, in ascending order, with a pattern of:

$\hat{1}$ whole step $\hat{2}$ whole step $\hat{3}$ half step $\hat{4}$

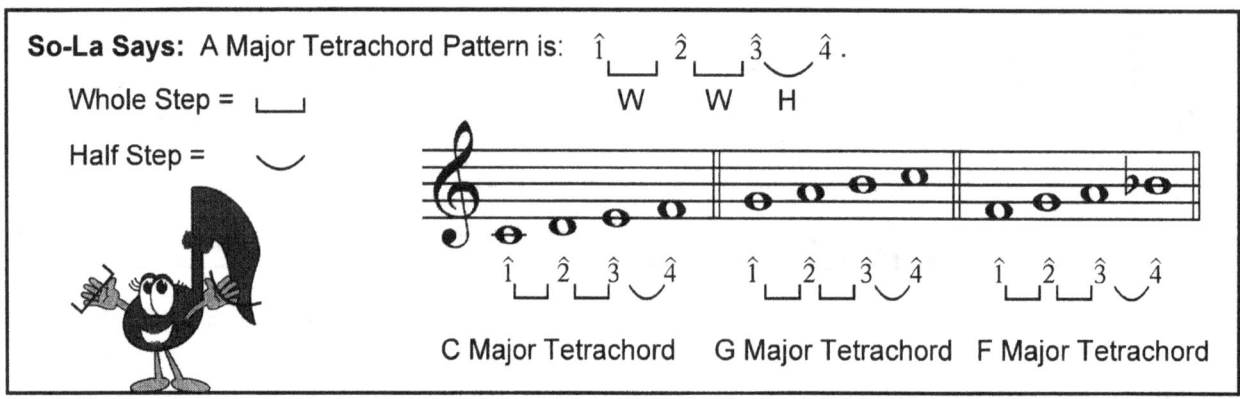

♫ **Ti-Do Tip:** Connect the Whole Step with a square bracket and the Half Step with a semitone-slur.

1. Identify the distance between the notes as ⌐⌐ for a Whole Step and as ⌣ for a Half Step.

2. a) Add the missing note to complete each Major Tetrachord. Use whole notes.
   b) Name each Major Tetrachord.

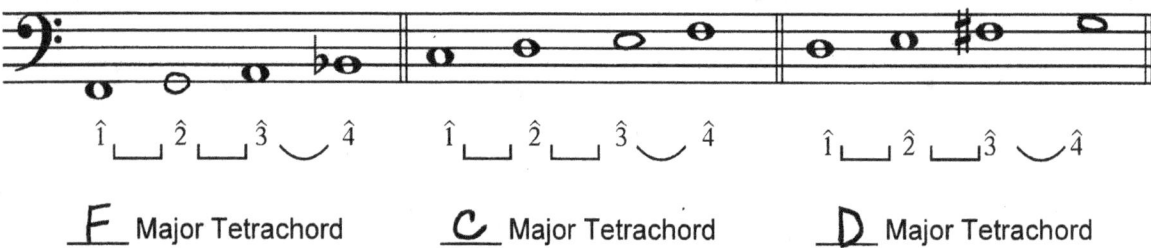

F Major Tetrachord   C Major Tetrachord   D Major Tetrachord

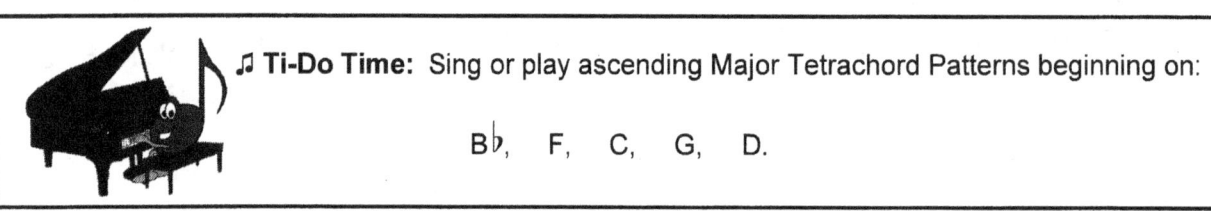

UltimateMusicTheory.com © Copyright 2017 Gloryland Publishing. All Rights Reserved.

MAJOR SCALES using ACCIDENTALS

A **Major Scale** is a pattern of two Major Tetrachords separated by a whole step.

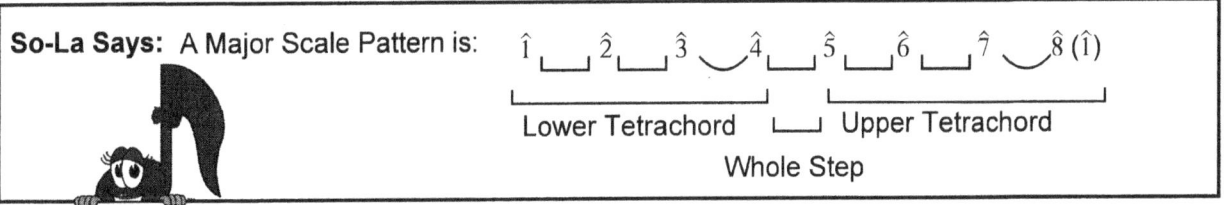

1. a) For the G Major Scale pattern, connect the whole steps with a square bracket. Connect the half steps with a semitone-slur.
   b) Identify the Lower Tetrachord and the Upper Tetrachord.

Lower Tetrachord   Whole Step   Upper Tetrachord

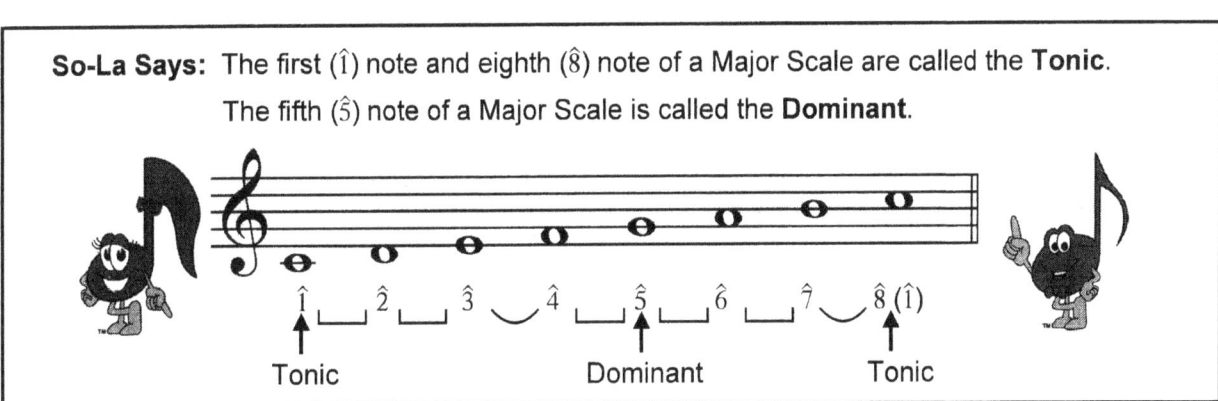

So-La Says: The first ($\hat{1}$) note and eighth ($\hat{8}$) note of a Major Scale are called the **Tonic**. The fifth ($\hat{5}$) note of a Major Scale is called the **Dominant**.

♪ **Ti-Do Tip:** The first ($\hat{1}$) note is the Lower Tonic. The eighth ($\hat{8}$) note is the Upper Tonic. They have the same Letter Name.

2. a) For the F Major Scale pattern, connect the whole steps with a square bracket. Connect the half steps with a semitone-slur.
   b) Identify the Tonic Notes with a T and the Dominant Note with a D.

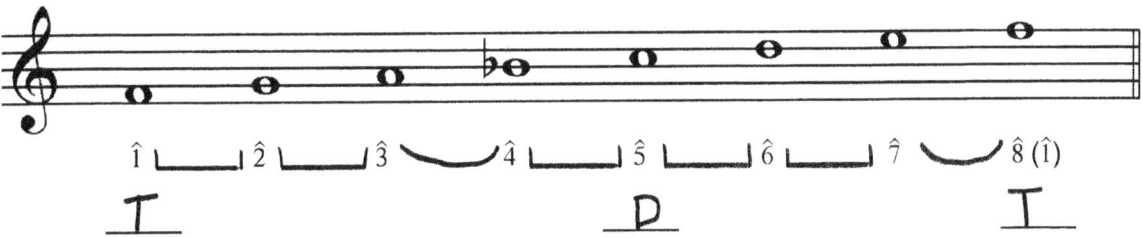

T   D   T

KEY SIGNATURES

A **Key Signature** is a sharp (or sharps) or a flat (or flats) from the Major Scale Pattern that is placed in a specific location at the beginning of the staff.

The C Major Scale Pattern has no sharps or flats. The **Key Signature of C Major** is no sharps/flats.

The G Major Scale Pattern has 1 sharp - F#. The **Key Signature of G Major** is 1 sharp - F#.

The F Major Scale Pattern has 1 flat - B♭. The **Key Signature of F Major** is 1 flat - B♭.

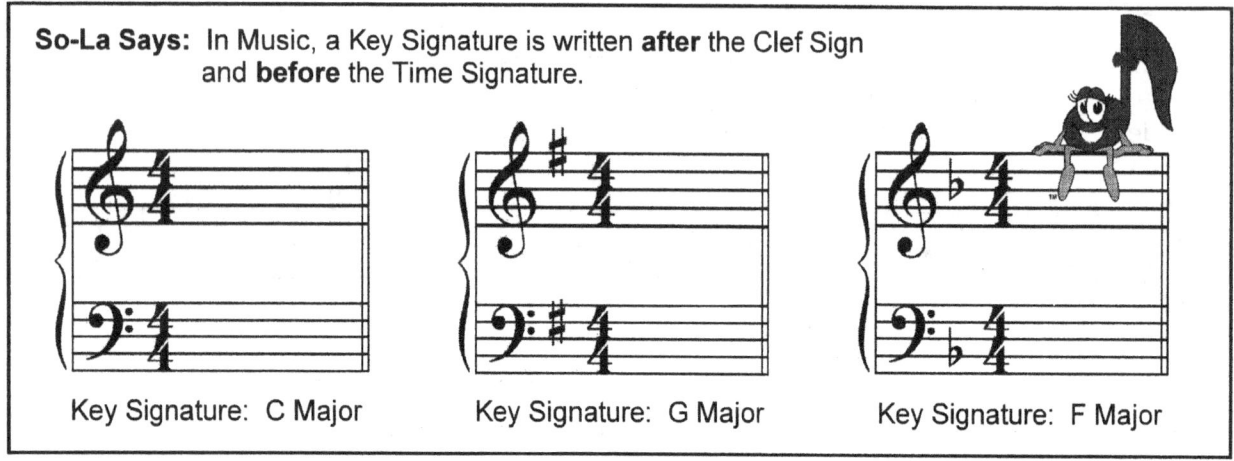

So-La Says: In Music, a Key Signature is written **after** the Clef Sign and **before** the Time Signature.

Key Signature: C Major | Key Signature: G Major | Key Signature: F Major

♪ **Ti-Do Tip:** A sharp or flat in the Key Signature affects **all** the notes with the **same letter name**.

1. a) Identify the ascending and descending Major Scale.
   b) Circle the notes affected by the Key Signature.
   c) Below the Staff, identify the Tonic Notes with a T and the Dominant Notes with a D.

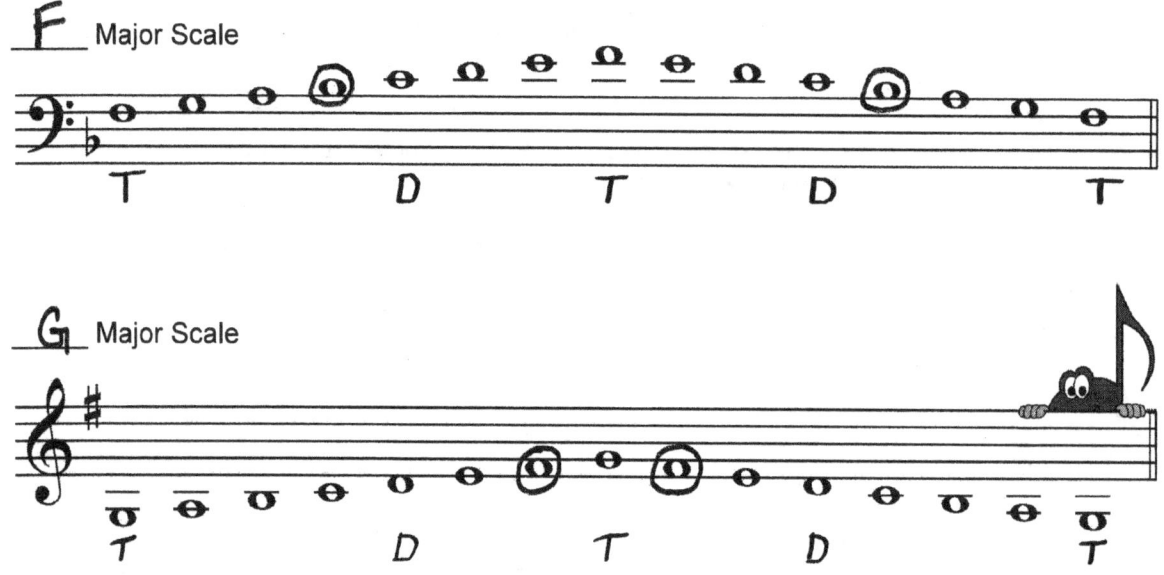

MAJOR SCALES with KEY SIGNATURES

The **G Major Scale Pattern** has an F♯. Instead of writing the sharp as an accidental in the scale, the sharp can be written at the beginning of the staff in the **Key Signature**.

So-La Says: G Major Scale with an **Accidental**.   G Major Scale with a **Key Signature**.

1. a) Write the G Major Scale ascending and descending one octave in the Treble Staff. Use a Key Signature. Use whole notes.
   b) Circle the notes affected by the Key Signature.

The **F Major Scale Pattern** has a B♭. Instead of writing the flat as an accidental in the scale, the flat can be written at the beginning of the staff in the **Key Signature**.

So-La Says: F Major Scale with an **Accidental**.   F Major Scale with a **Key Signature**.

2. a) Write the F Major Scale ascending and descending one octave in the Treble Staff. Use a Key Signature. Use whole notes.
   b) Circle the notes affected by the Key Signature.

♪ **Ti-Do Time:**   PLAY the Major Scale with an Accidental on your instrument. Then play the Major Scale with a Key Signature.

LISTEN as you play. Identify if the sound (what your hear) is the same or different when you play the Scales with Accidentals or with a Key Signature.

MINOR SCALE - NATURAL FORM

Each Major scale has a **relative minor scale** that starts on the sixth ($\hat{6}$) note of the Major scale.

The relative minor scale of C Major is a minor.

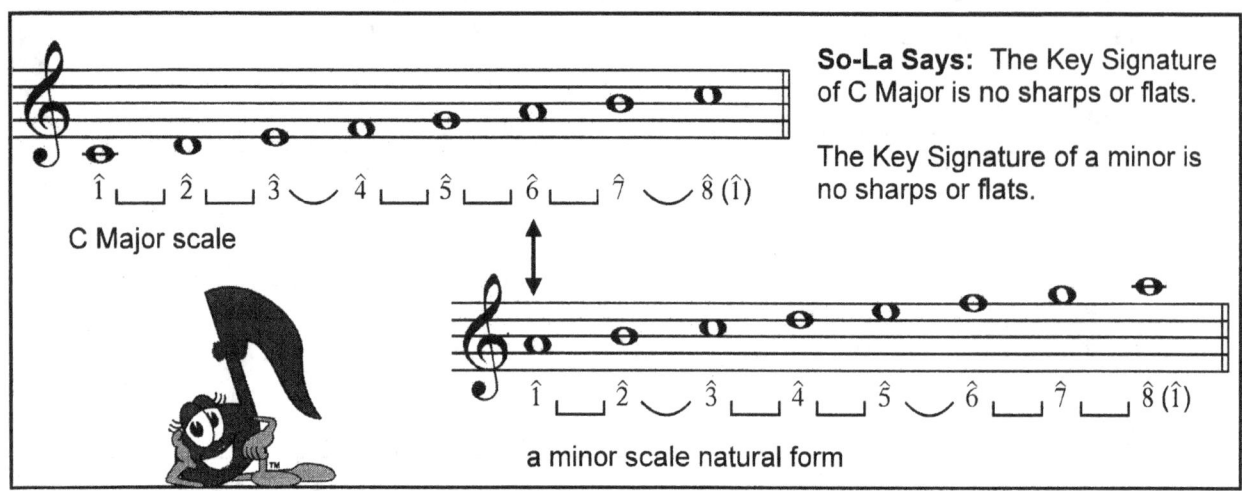

♪ **Ti-Do Tip:** The natural minor scale pattern is: $\hat{1}$ ⌐⌐ $\hat{2}$ ⌣ $\hat{3}$ ⌐⌐ $\hat{4}$ ⌐⌐ $\hat{5}$ ⌣ $\hat{6}$ ⌐⌐ $\hat{7}$ ⌐⌐ $\hat{8}(\hat{1})$.

1. a) Write the C Major scale ascending and descending. Use whole notes.
   b) Number the scale degrees.
   c) Connect the whole steps with a square bracket and the half steps with a semitone-slur.

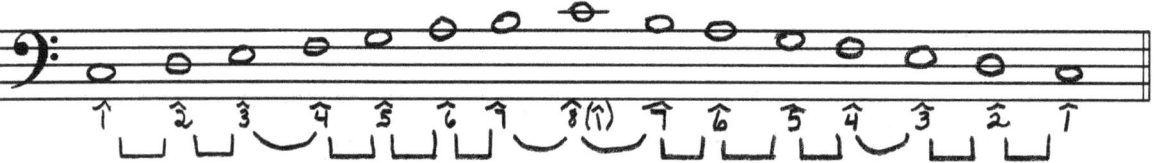

2. a) Write the a minor scale natural form ascending and descending. Use whole notes.
   b) Number the scale degrees.
   c) Connect the whole steps with a square bracket and the half steps with a semitone-slur.

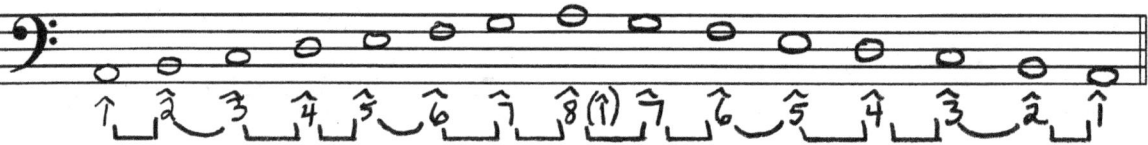

♪ **Ti-Do Time:** LISTEN as your Teacher plays the C Major scale or the a minor scale natural form, ascending and descending.

Identify if the scale (sound) is the Major scale sound or the minor scale sound.

TONIC TRIADS - SOLID/BLOCKED and BROKEN

The **Tonic Triad** is a three note chord using the following degrees (notes) of the Major or minor scale: Tonic (Root) $\hat{1}$, Mediant (Third) $\hat{3}$ and Dominant (Fifth) $\hat{5}$.

When the lowest note of the triad is the Root, the Triad is in Root Position.

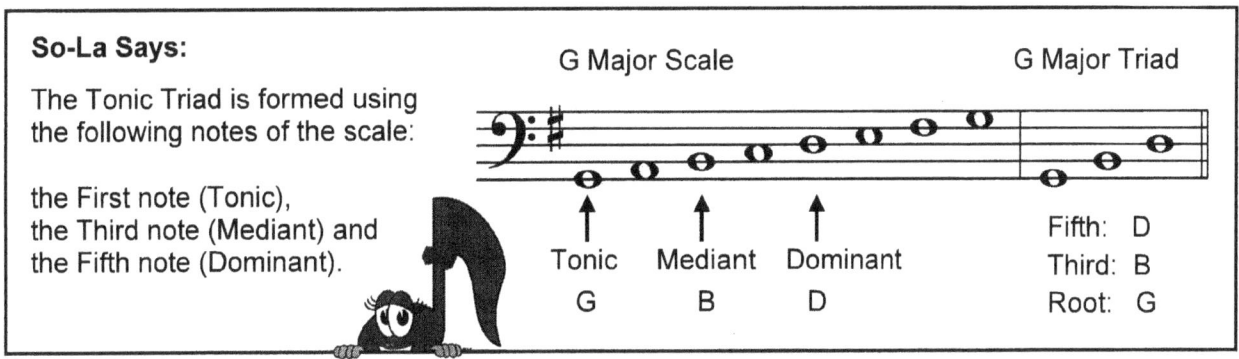

1. a) In Measure 1, write the C Major scale ascending one octave. Use whole notes.
   b) In Measure 2, write the notes of the C Major Tonic Triad ascending. Use whole notes.

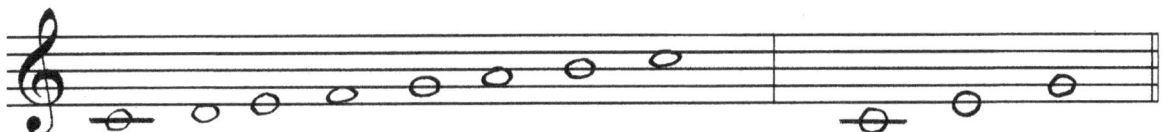

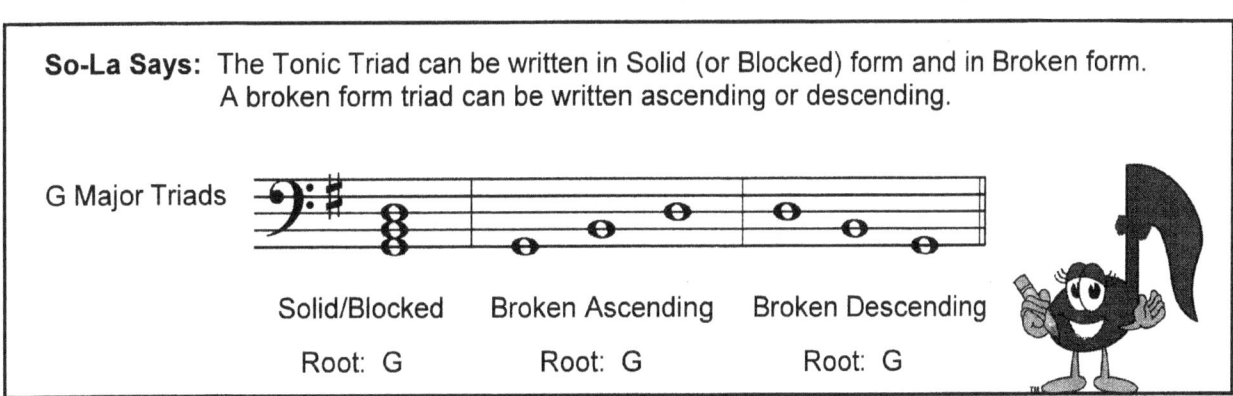

♪ **Ti-Do Tip:** The Root of a Tonic Triad is always the Tonic note.

2. Identify the Root Note of the following Root Position triads.

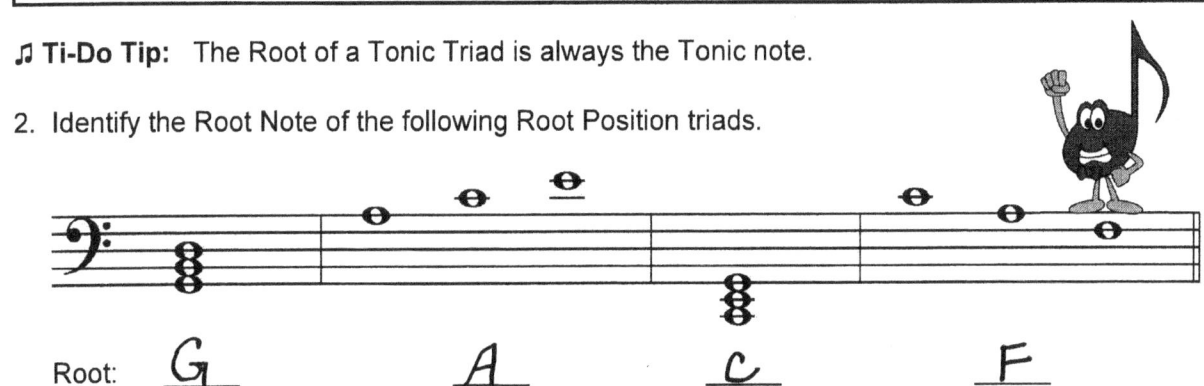

Root: G   A   C   F

COMMON TIME and TIED NOTES

4/4 Time is also known as **Common Time**. The symbol for Common Time is **C**.

> **So-La Says:** The Time Signature is written once at the beginning of the first measure, after the clef.
>
> Common Time **C** is the same as 4/4.
>
> Four beats per measure and a Quarter note equals one beat.

♪ **Ti-Do Tip:** The symbol for Common Time **C** is written in space two and space three on the staff.

1. Write the symbol for Common Time ("**C**") below the bracket for each measure of Common Time.

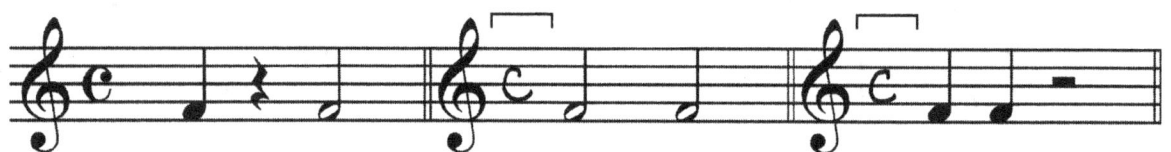

A **TIE** (curved line) connects two notes of the same pitch. The first note is played and held for the combined value of both tied notes. Ties usually occur between notes in neighbouring measures.

> **So-La Says:** A tie is written close to the notehead and away from the stems.

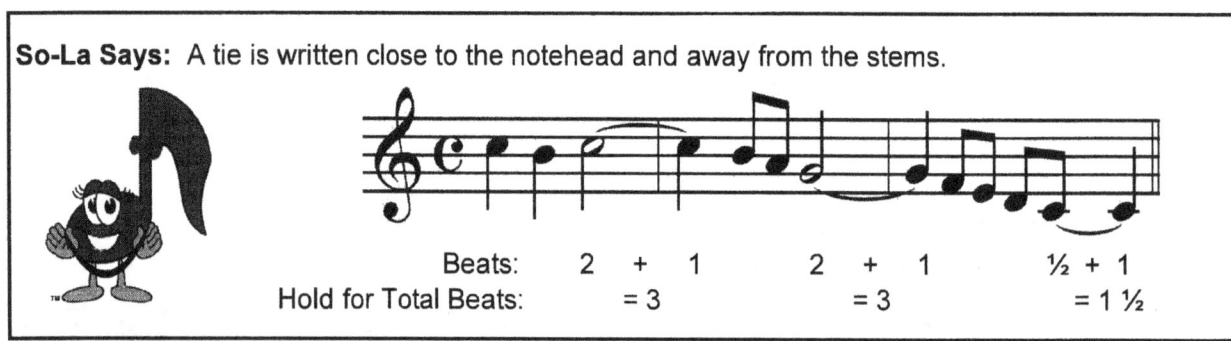

2. a) Write the number of beats each tied note receives.
   b) Write the total beats for the combined value of the tied notes.

Beats: 2 + 1   1½ + 1   2 + 2

Total Beats: = 3   = 1½   = 4

Bunk Bed Bar Lines!

So-La Says: Climb down the Bunk Bed ladder.

In each bunk bed, add bar lines.

For the rest and note in each pillow, answer the question. Observe the Time Signature!

In Common Time write the:

Number of beats the quarter rest receives. __1__

Number of beats the quarter note receives. __1__

In ¾ Time write the:

Number of beats the whole rest receives. __3__

Number of beats the dotted half note receives. __3__

In 2/4 Time write the:

Number of beats the eighth rest receives. __½__

Number of beats the eighth note receives. __½__

MOTIVE - RHYTHMIC PATTERN (Note Values) and MELODIC PATTERN (Intervals/Direction)

A **motive** is a short musical idea that can have a repeated Motive Pattern. The Motive Pattern may repeat the rhythm (rhythmic motive), melody (melodic motive) or both (melodic/rhythmic pattern).

♫ **Ti-Do Tip:** A melody may be written with a repeated rhythmic motive.
SAME Rhythmic Pattern (Note Values) - DIFFERENT Melodic Pattern (Intervals)

1. The motive below has a repeated rhythmic pattern in measures 1, 2 and 3 (the melodic pattern is different). Clap the rhythmic pattern in measures 1 to 4. Check (✓) the correct answer.

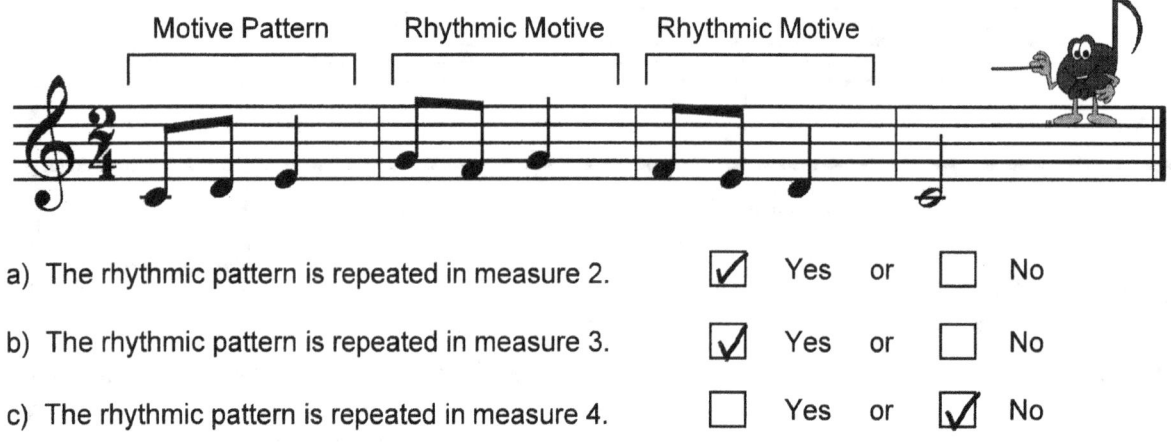

a) The rhythmic pattern is repeated in measure 2.   ☑ Yes or ☐ No

b) The rhythmic pattern is repeated in measure 3.   ☑ Yes or ☐ No

c) The rhythmic pattern is repeated in measure 4.   ☐ Yes or ☑ No

 **So-La Says:** A melody may repeat the melodic motive pattern at the same pitch or at a different (higher or lower) pitch, with the same rhythmic pattern.

♫ **Ti-Do Tip:** A melody may be written with a repeated melodic (and rhythmic) motive.
SAME Melodic Pattern (Intervals) - SAME Rhythmic Pattern (Note Values)

2. The motive below has a repeated melodic pattern in measures 1, 2 and 3 (the rhythmic pattern is also repeated). Sing the melodic pattern in measures 1 to 4. Check (✓) the correct answer.

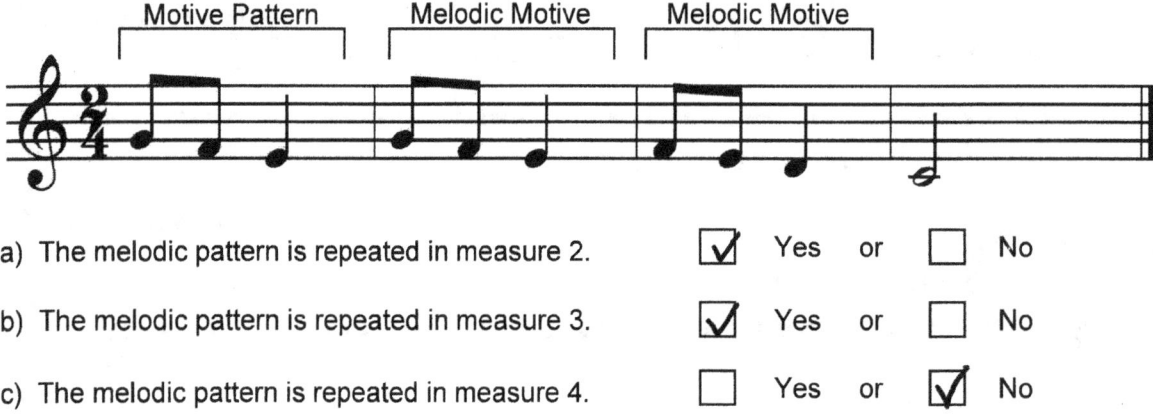

a) The melodic pattern is repeated in measure 2.   ☑ Yes or ☐ No

b) The melodic pattern is repeated in measure 3.   ☑ Yes or ☐ No

c) The melodic pattern is repeated in measure 4.   ☐ Yes or ☑ No

REPEATED MOTIVE - IDENTIFYING PATTERNS

♪ **Ti-Do Tip:** A melody may use a **Repeated Motive**. The motive may be repeated as:
Same Rhythmic Pattern + Different Melodic Pattern = **rhythmic motive** pattern OR
Same Rhythmic Pattern + Same Melodic pattern = **melodic/rhythmic motive** pattern.

1. For each melody, CIRCLE if the repeated pattern is a rhythmic motive or melodic/rhythmic motive.

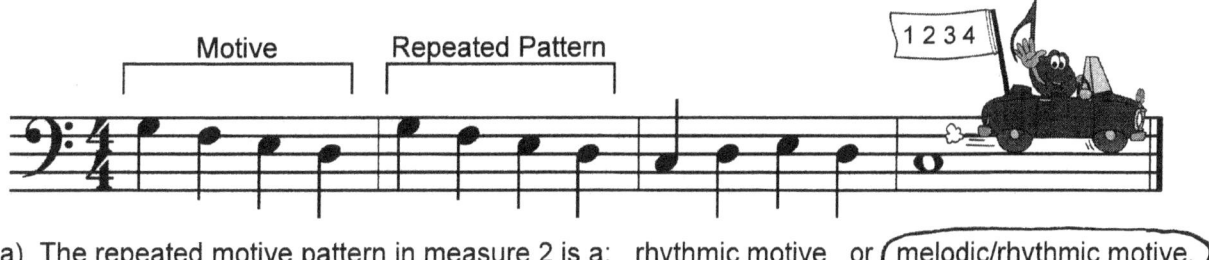

a) The repeated motive pattern in measure 2 is a: rhythmic motive or (melodic/rhythmic motive.)

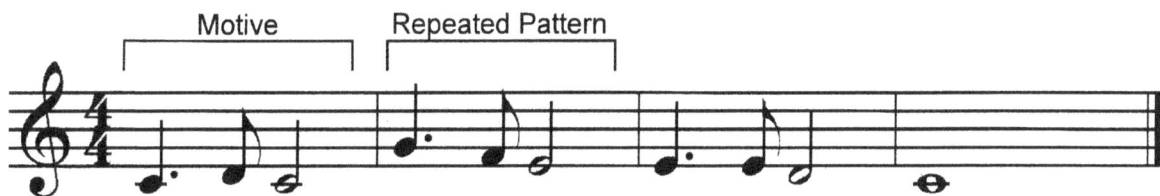

b) The repeated motive pattern in measure 2 is a: (rhythmic motive) or melodic/rhythmic motive.

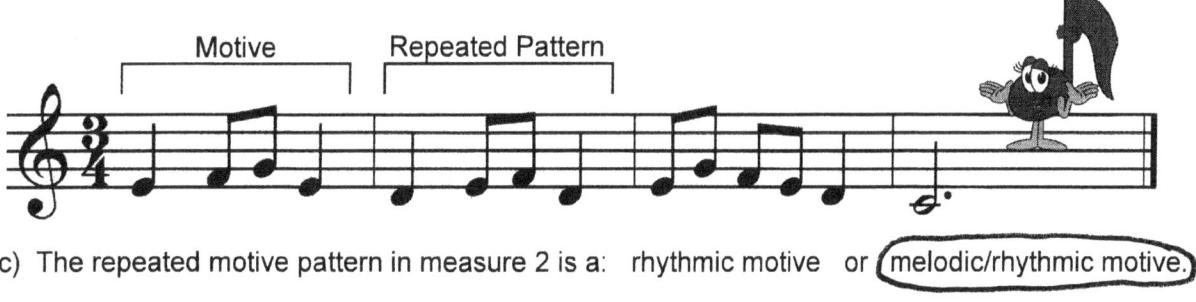

c) The repeated motive pattern in measure 2 is a: rhythmic motive or (melodic/rhythmic motive.)

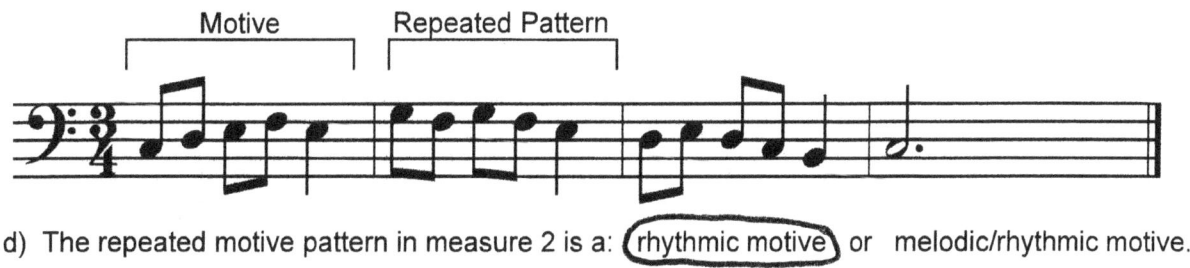

d) The repeated motive pattern in measure 2 is a: (rhythmic motive) or melodic/rhythmic motive.

COMPOSING - RHYTHMIC PATTERNS

A Melody may have a repeated **Rhythmic Pattern**. A rhythmic pattern is a set of beats and/or rests that create the pulse of the music. This rhythmic sound may be repeated in the music.

♫ **Ti-Do Tip:** A melody may use the same rhythmic pattern repeated in the music.

1. a) Copy the rhythmic pattern from measure 1 into measure 2 (at the same pitch).
   b) Copy the rhythmic pattern from measure 3 into measure 4 (at the same pitch).
   c) Clap the rhythm. Listen for the repeated rhythmic patterns.

So-La Says: When a rhythmic pattern is repeated in a melody, the melodic pattern (melody) may use notes at a different pitch. Same Rhythm - Different Pitch

2. a) Compose a melody in measure 2 using the same rhythmic pattern from measure 1. Use notes at a different pitch - different melodic pattern. Move by step or repeated notes.
   b) Play the melody on your instrument. Listen for the repeated rhythmic patterns.

(one possible answer)

3. a) The melody below is in C Major. Compose a melody in measure 1. Start on the Tonic Note. Use the given rhythm. Move by step or repeated notes.
   b) Compose a melody in measure 2 using the same rhythmic pattern from measure 1. Use notes at a different pitch - different melodic pattern. Move by step or repeated notes.

(one possible answer)

COMPOSING - MELODIC PATTERNS

A Melody may have a repeated **Melodic Pattern**. A melodic pattern is a set of notes (moving up, down or repeated) that create the melody. This melodic sound may be repeated in the music.

♫ **Ti-Do Tip:** A melody may use the same melodic and rhythmic pattern repeated in the music.

1. a) Copy the melodic pattern from measure 1 into measure 2 (at the same pitch).
   b) Copy the melodic pattern from measure 3 into measure 4 (at the same pitch).
   c) Play the melody on your instrument. Listen for the repeated melodic patterns.

So-La Says: When a melodic pattern is repeated in a melody, the melodic pattern may begin on the same pitch or on a different pitch. Same Melody - Same and/or Different Pitch

2. The melodic pattern in measure 1 is repeated in measure 2 beginning one step higher in pitch.

   a) Compose a melody in measure 3 using the same melodic pattern from measure 2. Begin one step higher in pitch. Use the given rhythm.
   b) Play the melody on your instrument. Listen for the repeated melodic patterns.

3. a) Compose a melody in measure 2 and measure 3. Use the same melodic pattern as measure 1. Begin each melodic pattern on a different pitch (one step higher or one step lower).
   b) Play the melody on your instrument. Listen for the repeated melodic and rhythmic patterns.

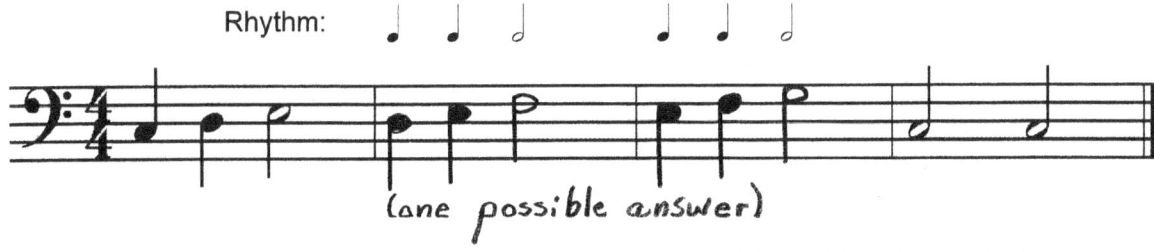

(one possible answer)

MELODY WRITING - REPEATED NOTES & STEPWISE MOTION

A Melody may be composed of **repeated notes** and notes moving in **stepwise motion** (up or down).

> **So-La Says:** Beethoven's "Ode to Joy" motive is heard in the final movement of his Symphony No. 9. Beethoven used repeated notes and notes moving in stepwise motion.

1. This melody is in the key of C Major. Play the melody on your instrument.

a) Circle all the groups of two repeated notes. There are __4__ groups of repeated notes.

b) Circle if the stepwise pattern of the melody at the letter A is: (stepping up) or stepping down.

c) Circle if the stepwise pattern of the melody at the letter B is: stepping up or (stepping down).

d) The melody ends on the Tonic note __C__. The Tonic note is played __4__ times.

♪ **Ti-Do Tip:** A melody may be based on the notes of a Major Scale. A melody that ends on the Tonic note (stable degree 1̂) sounds finished, like the period at the end of a sentence.

2. Compose two melodies in C Major, one in the Treble Clef and one in the Bass Clef. Use the given rhythm. Use repeated notes and notes moving by step (up or down). End on the Tonic note C.

MELODY WRITING - KEY SIGNATURES & TIME SIGNATURES

A Melody may be composed of notes from a Major scale using the **Key Signature** of the Major key.
A Melody is written with a **Time Signature** to indicate the rhythmic pulse of the melody.

So-La Says: When writing a melody, the Key Signature is written after the Clef.
The Time Signature is written after the Key Signature.

Clef - Key Signature - Time Signature

1. Compose a melody in G Major. Use repeated notes and notes moving by step (up or down). Use the given rhythm. End on the Tonic note G (stable degree $\hat{1}$ of the G Major scale).

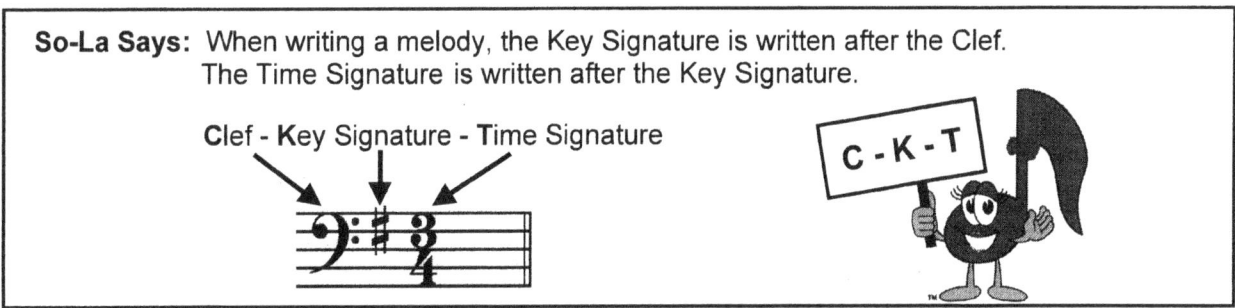

(one possible answer)

♫ **Ti-Do Tip:** A double bar line indicates the end of the music. When writing double bar lines at the end of a melody, use two thin bar lines written close together.

1. Compose two melodies in F Major. Use repeated notes and notes moving by step (up or down). Use the given rhythm. End on the Tonic note (of F Major). Draw a double bar line at the end.

(one possible answer)

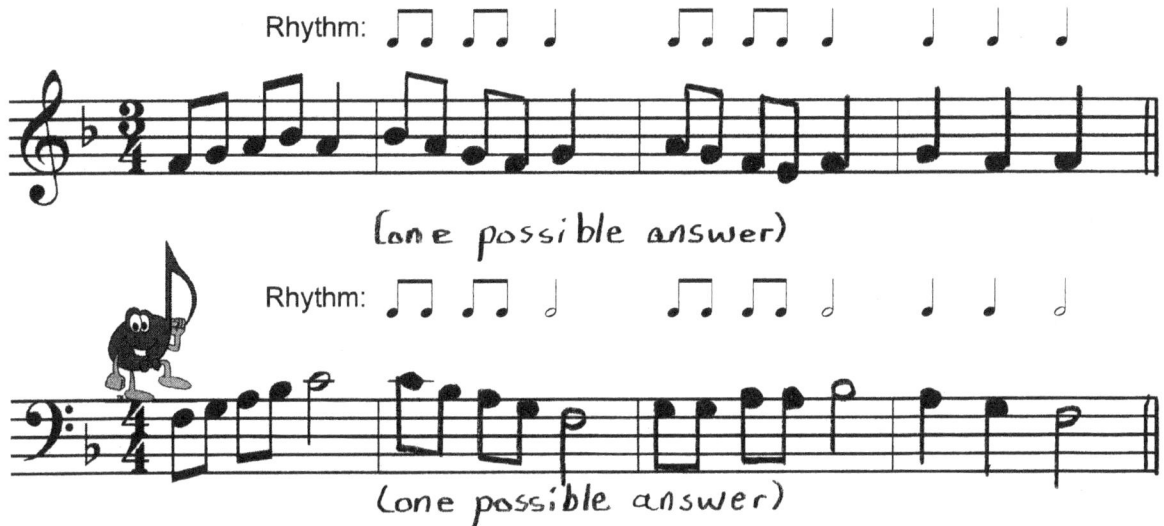

(one possible answer)

IMAGINE, COMPOSE, EXPLORE

Composing, or melody writing, means to create new music. After you compose your music, sing or play your composition on your instrument.

♪ **I**magine the music telling a story or idea. The title (written at the top) describes the composition.
♪ **C**ompose your musical idea. The name (written at the top right) identifies the composer.
♪ **E**xplore the music. Add "So-La Sparkles" using dynamics and articulation to enhance the sound.

> **So-La Says:** First compose freely without writing anything down. Use a recording device (such as your phone, computer or video camera) to record yourself. HAVE FUN!
>
> Use the recording to assist you in writing out your composition. Use different dynamics, articulation and tempo to create different sounds and adventures.

1. For each of the following: compose a melody in measures 2, 3 & 4. Use the given rhythm.

   a) Imagine your musical idea by completing the title at the top. Write your name as the composer.
   b) Compose a melody using repeated notes or notes that move by step. End on the Tonic 1̂ note.
   c) Explore the music. Add "So-La Sparkles" using dynamics and articulation. Play your piece.
   (one possible answer)

ANALYSIS, MUSICAL TERMS and SIGHT READING

Analysis of a piece is the process of identifying composition details including **Musical Terms**.

Musical Term	Definition
accelerando, accel.	becoming quicker
a tempo	return to the original tempo
ritardando (rit.)	slowing down gradually

♫ **Ti-Do Tip:** Musical Terms indicate details from the composer to show how a piece is to be played.

1. Analyze the piece of music by answering the questions below.

   a) Identify and explain the Time Signature. <u>Common Time   4 Beats per measure   ♩ = 1 Beat</u>

   b) Is the rhythmic pattern of the motive in measure 1 repeated in measure 2? <u>Yes</u>

   c) Explain the term rit. in measure 6. <u>ritardando - slowing down gradually</u>

   d) Identify the melodic interval (numerical size) at the letter A. <u>second</u>

   e) Identify the total value of the tied notes at the letter B. <u>8 beats</u>

♫ **Ti-Do Time:** PLAY (Sight Read) the "Brave Little Mouse" on your instrument. Observe all the Musical Terms and Signs. Have Fun and Be Brave!

ORCHESTRAL INSTRUMENTS

An Orchestra is a large group of musicians performing together on String, Woodwind, Brass and Percussion instruments. The **Orchestra Instruments** are divided into sections.

Orchestra Sections:

Strings (violin, viola, cello and double bass) are arranged at the front;

Woodwinds (flute, oboe, clarinet and bassoon) are arranged behind the strings;

Brass (French horn, trumpet, trombone and tuba) are also arranged behind the strings;

Percussion (timpani, cymbals, triangle, snare drum, bass drum, xylophone & harp) are at the back and

Other (piano & glass harmonica) may also be used.

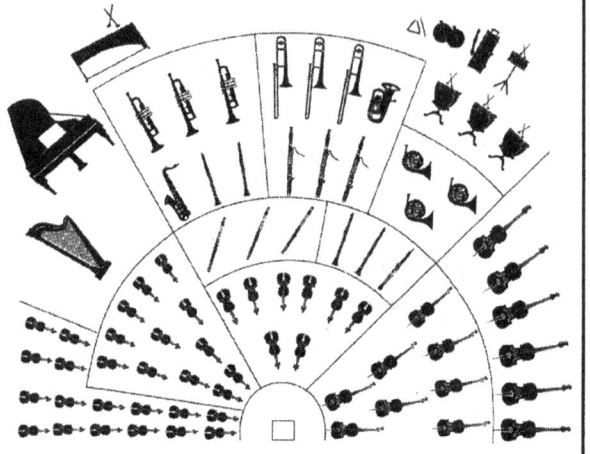

Instruments in the String Family are made of wood or metal, and have strings. The strings vibrate and create sound. The hollow body of the instrument acts as a resonator to control the dynamics.

Instruments in the Woodwind Family are divided into 2 main sections: In section one, players blow across the tip of a tube. In section two, players blow into 1 or more reeds (thin strips of cane).

Instruments in the Brass Family create sound when the player blows into the mouthpiece. The way the player vibrates their lips against the mouthpiece is called their "embouchure".

Instruments in the Percussion Family create sound when they are hit, scraped, rubbed, shaken or whirled. This is the largest family of instruments and range in size from tiny sleigh bells to huge bells.

1. Draw a line to match the instruments with their correct orchestral section.

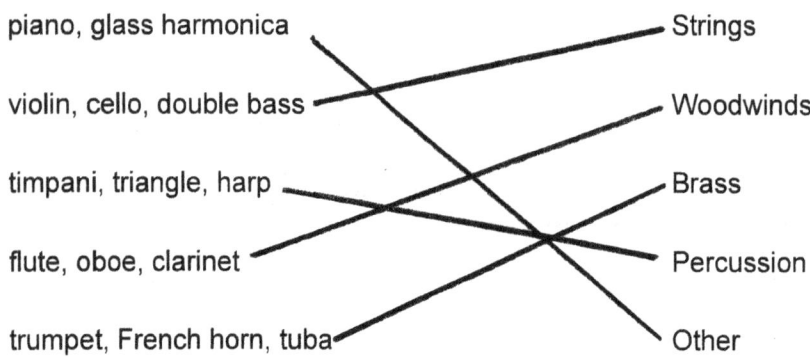

UltimateMusicTheory.com © Copyright 2017 Gloryland Publishing. All Rights Reserved.

STORY TELLING THROUGH SOUND

The instruments in the orchestra create **sound** that help us imagine **story telling**. Instruments also create sound effects for movies and concerts! Each instrument has a unique sound and pitch range.

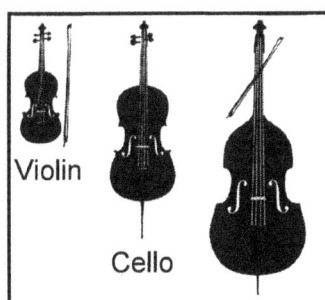

The **Violin**, **Cello** and **Double Bass** belong to the String Family.

They are played with a bow or by plucking the strings with fingers (called pizzicato). Shorter strings = higher sound; longer strings = lower sound.

A Violin is usually 23-24 inches long. It makes high (soprano) sounds.
A Cello is usually 3-4 feet tall. It makes middle/low (tenor/bass) sounds.
A Double Bass is 6 feet tall. It makes low (bass) sounds.

1. The Violin, Cello and Double Bass belong to the __string__ family of instruments.

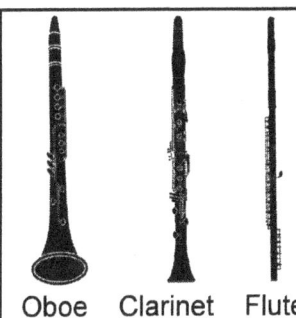

The **Oboe**, **Clarinet** and **Flute** belong to the Woodwind Family.

Instruments in the Woodwind Family are not all made from wood! They are also made from clay, metal, glass, ivory and plastics.

An Oboe uses 2 reeds (double reed) to create high (nasal) sounds.
A Clarinet uses 1 reed (single reed) to create low to high sounds.
A Flute is made of silver or wood to create high (soprano) sounds.

2. The Oboe, Clarinet and Flute belong to the __woodwind__ family of instruments.

Instruments, such as the Glass Armonica, that do not create sound using the definitions of the four main Instrument Families are found in the "**Other Instruments**" section of the Orchestra.

The **Glass Armonica**, or **Glass Harmonica**, was invented by Benjamin Franklin in 1761. "A*rmonia*" is the Italian word for harmony.

The Glass Armonica is a spinning instrument made from glass bowls and played with wet fingertips. It creates unique sweet and soft sounds.

3. The Glass Armonica is also called the __Glass__ __Harmonica__.

Watch, Listen, Learn: Go to **GSGmusic.com** to watch the videos and hear how instruments sound.

STORY TELLING through MUSIC - PETER and the WOLF

Peter and the Wolf is a "fairy tale" for Symphony Orchestra and narrator, written in 1936 by Russian composer Sergei Prokofiev (1891 - 1953). His Mother taught him to play the piano. She also encouraged him to imagine, compose and explore the piano by making up his own songs.

Sergei Prokofiev, known as the greatest of all Russian Composers, was born in the village of Sontzovka in southern European Russia.

By the age of 9, he had written a three-act Opera called "The Giant". He wrote many operas, ballets, symphonies and concertos for piano, violin and cello.

One of his most popular musical works, composed especially for children, was the story and the music of Peter and the Wolf.

Peter and the Wolf is a story about a boy named Peter, who opens the gate and walks out into the meadow. There, on a branch, Peter meets his friend the Bird. The story continues with the arrival of the Duck, the Cat, the Grandfather and of course the Wolf! Eventually they are joined by the Hunters!

The music helps tell the story as each character is represented by a specific instrument. The instruments create unique sounds that help us imagine each character as the story unfolds.

To answer the questions below, listen to the story and the music of Peter and the Wolf.

Go to **GSGMUSIC.com** - For Easy Access to Videos for Listening to Peter and the Wolf.

1. Enjoy listening to the story and the music of Peter and the Wolf. Listen for: Peter and the Bird. Check (✓) the correct answer to the questions below.

The sound of **Peter** is created by the String Family. (Violin, Viola, Cello & Double Bass)

Is Peter brave or scared to go into the woods? ☑ Brave or ☐ Scared

The sound of the **Bird** is created by the Flute.

What pitch is the chirping sound of the Bird? ☐ Low or ☑ High

STORY TELLING through MUSIC - PETER and the WOLF

1. Continue listening to Peter and the Wolf. Listen for: the Duck, the Cat, the Grandfather, the Wolf and the Hunters. Check (✓) the correct answer to the questions below.

The sound of the **Duck** is created by the Oboe.

What is the tempo of the waddling Duck? ☐ Fast or ☑ Slow

The sound of the **Cat** is created by the Clarinet.

What is the dynamic when the Cat is sneaking up? ☑ Piano or ☐ Forte

The sound of the **Grandfather** is created by the Bassoon.

Was the Grandfather happy or angry at Peter? ☐ Happy or ☑ Angry

The sound of the **Wolf** is created by three French Horns.

Did the Wolf swallow the Duck or the Bird? ☑ Duck or ☐ Bird

The sounds of the **Hunters Gun Shots** are created by the Timpani Drums.

Where did Peter want the Hunters to take the Wolf? ☐ Woods or ☑ Zoo

STORY TELLING through MUSIC - CARNIVAL of the ANIMALS

Carnival of the Animals is a musical parade of 14 short humorous pieces composed in 1886.

French composer Camille Saint-Saëns (1835 - 1921) began piano lessons at the age of 5 and started composing at the age of 6.

He composed Carnival of the Animals to explore the instrument families of the orchestra as they represent the March of the Lions, Hens and Roosters, Wild Horses, Tortoise, Elephant, Kangaroos, Aquarium, Donkeys, Cuckoo, Aviary, Pianist, Fossils, Swan and the Finale.

Go to **GSGMUSIC.com** - For Easy Access to Videos for Listening to Carnival of the Animals.

1. Enjoy listening to Carnival of the Animals. Listen for the: Elephant, Kangaroos, Aquarium and the Swan. Check (✓) the correct answer to the questions below.

The sound of the **Elephant** is created by the Double Bass.

At what tempo is the Elephant moving? ☐ Allegro   or   ✓ Lento

The sound of the **Kangaroos** is created by two Pianos.

What articulation is used for the Kangaroo? ✓ Staccato   or   ☐ Legato

Sounds in the **Aquarium** are created by the Glass Harmonica and other instruments.

What other instruments are used? ✓ Strings   or   ☐ Drums

The sound of the **Swan** is created by the Cello and the Piano.

What dynamic is the sound of the Swan? ☐ Forte   or   ✓ Piano

Ultimate Music Theory
Level 1 Theory Exam

Total Score: ____
           100

The Ultimate Music Theory™ Rudiments Workbooks, Supplemental Workbooks and Exams prepare students for successful completion of the Royal Conservatory of Music Theory Levels.

1. a) Name the following notes.
   b) Draw a line from each note to the corresponding key on the keyboard (at the correct pitch).

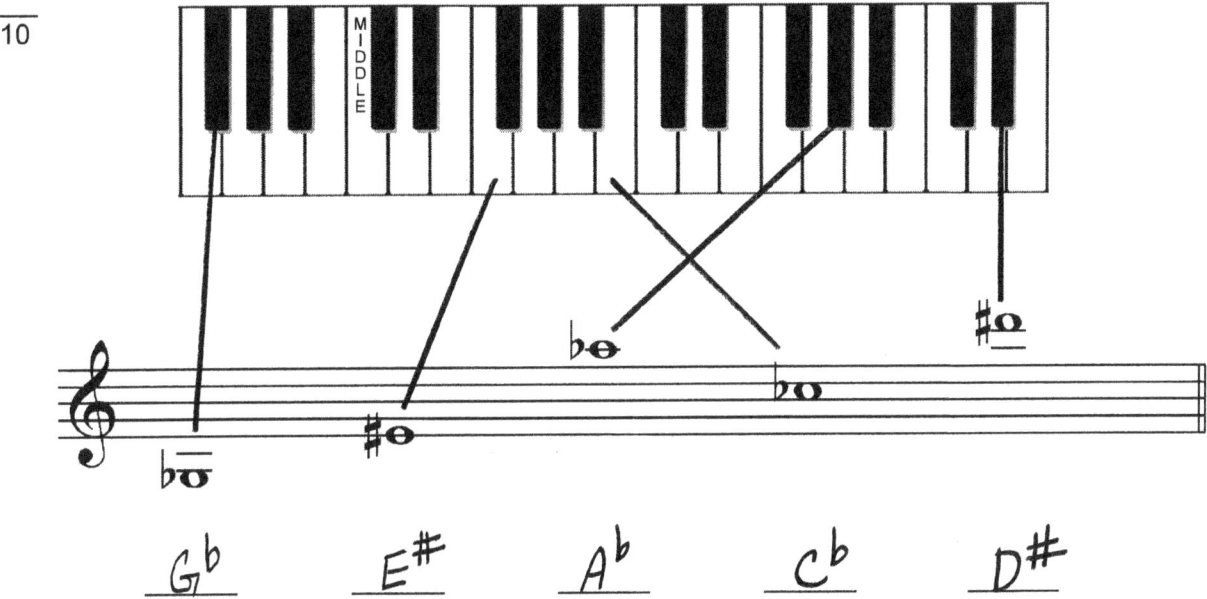

G♭   E♯   A♭   C♭   D♯

2. a) Write the note that is a half step (semitone) above each given note. Use the same letter name (chromatic). Use a whole note.

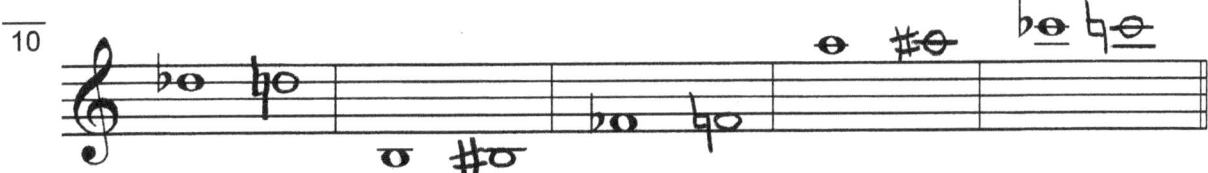

b) Write the note that is a half step (semitone) below each given note. Use a different letter name (diatonic). Use a whole note.

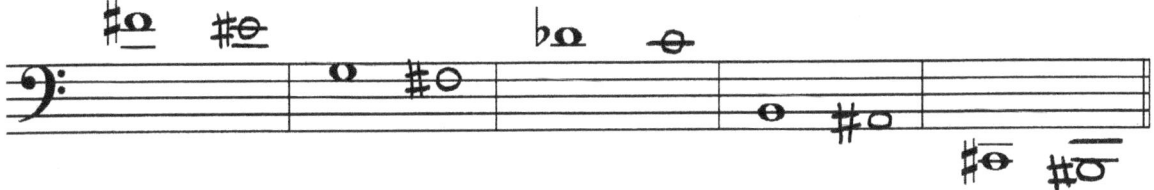

Ultimate Music Theory
Level 1 Theory Exam

3. Add bar lines to complete the following rhythms. Observe the Time Signatures.

4. For each of the following rhythms, add the correct Time Signature below the bracket.

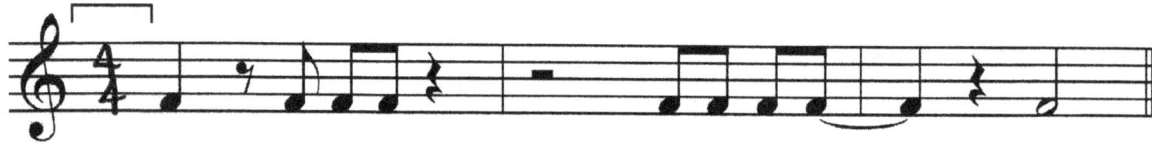

Ultimate Music Theory
Level 1 Theory Exam

5. Name the interval (numerical size only) below each bracket.

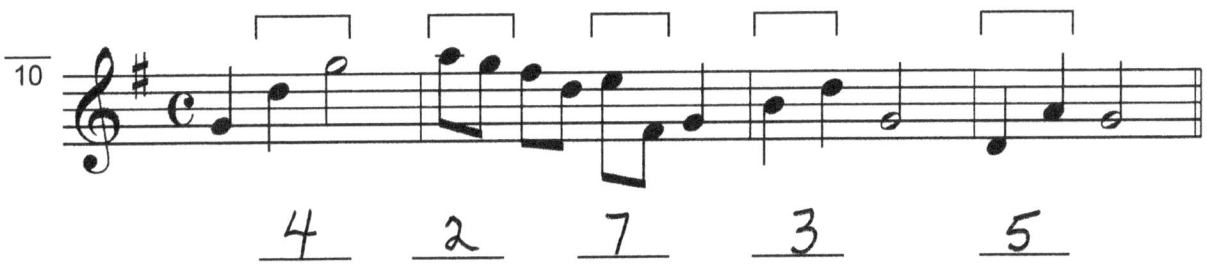

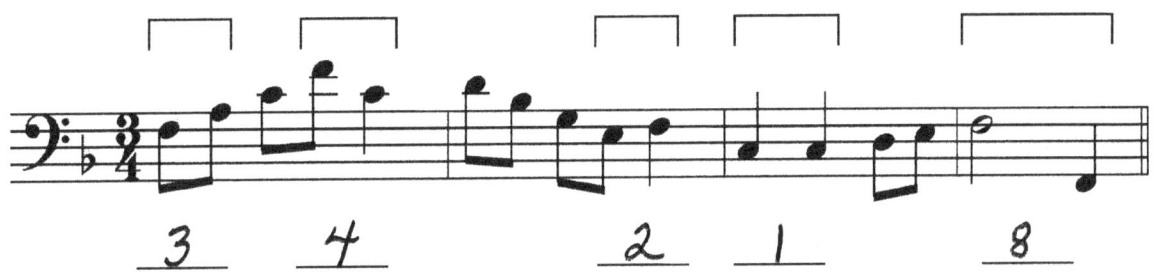

6. Match each musical term with the English definition. (Not all definitions will be used.)

Term		Definition
tempo	b	a) fast
ritardando, rit.	j	b) speed at which music is performed
fermata	h	c) becoming softer
andante	e	d) at a moderate tempo
a tempo	f	e) moderately slow, at a walking pace
allegro	a	f) return to the original tempo
moderato	d	g) becoming louder
tie	k	h) hold the note or rest longer than its written value
diminuendo, dim.	c	i) slow
lento	i	j) slowing down gradually
		k) hold for the combined value of the tied notes

Ultimate Music Theory
Level 1 Theory Exam

7. Circle the correct answer for each of the following.

   a) Carnival of the Animals was composed by:

   Sergei Prokofiev   or   (Camille Saint-Saëns)

   b) In Carnival of the Animals, the hopping sound of the Kangaroo is played by:

   (two Pianos)   or   two Cellos

   c) In Carnival of the Animals, the slow, lumbering sound of the Elephant is played by:

   the Trumpet   or   (the Double Bass)

   d) In Carnival of the Animals, the rippling water sound of the Aquarium is played by:

   (the Glass Harmonica)   or   the Tuba

   e) In Carnival of the Animals, the graceful gliding sound of the Swan is played by:

   the Drums and Oboe   or   (the Cello and Piano)

   f) Peter and the Wolf was composed by:

   (Sergei Prokofiev)   or   Camille Saint-Saëns

   g) In Peter and the Wolf, the creeping Cat sound is played by:

   (the Clarinet)   or   the Violin

   h) In Peter and the Wolf, the waddling Duck sound is played by:

   the Timpani Drums   or   (the Oboe)

   i) In Peter and the Wolf, the dangerous Wolf sound is played by:

   (Three French Horns)   or   Three Pianos

   j) In Peter and the Wolf, the playful skipping sound of Peter is played by:

   the Woodwinds   or   (the Strings)

Ultimate Music Theory
Level 1 Theory Exam

8. a) Write the G Major scale ascending and descending one octave. Use a Key Signature Use whole notes. Write T below each Tonic note. Write D below each Dominant note.

b) Write the F Major scale ascending and descending one octave. Use a Key Signature. Use whole notes. Write T below each Tonic note. Write D below each Dominant note.

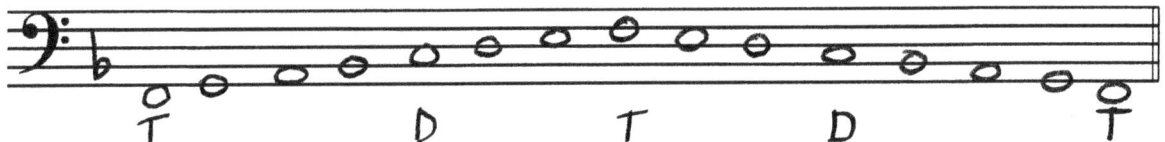

c) Add a Treble Clef or a Bass Clef at the beginning of the staff to form the C Major scale. Connect the half steps with a semitone-slur.

d) Add a Treble Clef or a Bass Clef at the beginning of the staff to form the a minor natural scale. Connect the half steps with a semitone-slur.

e) Add a Treble Clef or a Bass Clef at the beginning of the staff to form the G Major scale. Connect the half steps with a semitone-slur.

Ultimate Music Theory
Level 1 Theory Exam

9. Match each triad name with the correct triad.

10

G Major Triad, Solid (Blocked), in the Bass Clef   __c__   a)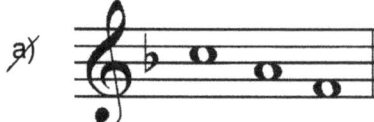

C Major Triad, Broken descending (going down), in the Bass Clef   __f__   b)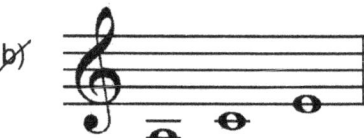

F Major Triad, Solid (Blocked), in the Treble Clef   __d__   c)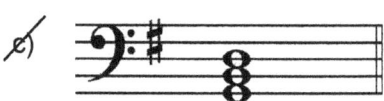

G Major Triad, Broken ascending (going up), in the Bass Clef   __e__   d)

F Triad, Broken descending (going down), in the Treble Clef   __a__   e)

a minor Triad, Broken ascending (going up), in the Treble Clef   __b__   f)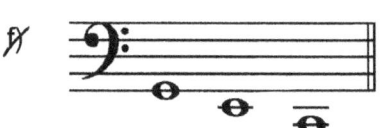

Ultimate Music Theory
Level 1 Theory Exam

10. Analyze the following piece of music by answering the questions below.

Magic Tricks

G. St. Germain

a) Name the title of this piece. __Magic Tricks__

b) Name the composer of this piece. __G. St. Germain__

c) Add the Time Signature directly on the music.

d) Explain the meaning of "*mp*". __mezzo piano - medium soft__

e) Name the root of the triad at the letter A. The root is __C__

f) Circle if the triad at the letter A is: (**solid (blocked)**) or broken

g) Circle if the rhythmic pattern in measure 1 is repeated in measure 2. Yes or (**No**)

h) Explain the sign at the letter B. __tied note - hold for combined value of the tied notes__

i) Explain the sign at the letter C. __fermata - hold, pause__

j) Magic Tricks is played fast. Circle if the tempo should be: (*allegro*) or *lento*

Bonus - Play "Magic Tricks" on your instrument. Have fun!

UltimateMusicTheory.com © Copyright 2017 Gloryland Publishing. All Rights Reserved. 47

Ultimate Music Theory Certificate

_____

has successfully completed all the requirements of the

Music Theory Level 1

_____   _____
Music Teacher   *Date*

Enriching Lives Through Music Education

www.ingramcontent.com/pod-product-compliance
Lightning Source LLC
Chambersburg PA
CBHW081734100526
44591CB00016B/2612